FOR REFERENCE

Do Not Take From This Room

Key Words in Judaism

Key Words in Judaism

Ron Geaves

Georgetown University Press / Washington, D.C.

As of January 1, 2007, 13-digit ISBN numbers will replace the current 10-digit system.
Paperback: 978-1-58901-128-1

Georgetown University Press, Washington, D.C.

This edition is published by arrangement with The Continuum International Publishing Group Ltd., London, U.K.

Library of Congress Cataloging-in-Publication Data

Geaves, Ron.
  Key words in Judaism / Ron Geaves.
     p. cm.
  ISBN 1-58901-128-7 (alk. paper)
  1. Judaism—Dictionaries. 2. Judaism—Terminology. I. Title.
  BM50.G43 2006
  296.03—dc22

                        2006006887

This book is printed on acid-free paper meeting the requirements of the American National Standard for Permanence in Paper for Printed Library Materials.

13 12 11 10 09 08 07 06   9 8 7 6 5 4 3 2
First printing

Printed in Great Britain

Contents

PREFACE

During the course of teaching a number of religions in four higher education institutions, one common feature has been the number of students who have expressed to me that they have experienced the mastering of religious terminology in so many unknown languages and also involving unfamiliar concepts to be the most daunting part of the module. In view of this, the *Key Words* series was created to provide a glossary of terms for five religions.

The religions have been chosen to reflect the main traditions that are studied both in school and at university in the English-speaking world. One glossary also contains the key specialist terminology used in the academic study of religion. It is hoped that the glossaries will prove to be useful and informative resources for anyone studying religion up to undergraduate level, but that they will also provide a fascinating pool of information for anyone interested in religious practice or belief, whether for the purpose of gaining qualifications or simply in personal pursuit of knowledge. Each glossary therefore provides an exhaustive exploration of religious terminology in a way that is accessible but also provides an overall in-depth understanding of the religious tradition.

Although Judaism is now provided with its own separate book, even so the glossary's completion remains arbitrary as each religion covered by the *Key Words* series commands a vast vocabulary that is a conceptual framework for viewing the world. This is true of Judaism, even though it is a relatively small religious tradition, as it has essentially maintained Hebrew as the language of religious expression and literature. Moreover, Judiasm is an ancient tradition with 5,000 years of history and during that period has experienced dramatic changes that have influenced and developed its religious vocabulary. The European diaspora also created an alternative language of Yiddish and I have included terms in that language which have entered popular usage. My choice of terms has been determined by school and undergraduate curricula, and the length of each definition has been dictated by the fact that this is a glossary and not a specialist religious dictionary. Inevitably, however, some concepts and persons needed more than a short passage in order to clarify their significance and highlight their importance within the world of their respective religion. I am aware of the variants in transliterating from Hebrew to English and have provided alternatives. The chosen spellings remain part of the spirit of the original glossary which was to provide acceptable variant spellings to non-specialists.

Finally, I would like to thank Catherine Barnes, whose patience and support has been remarkable; Janet Joyce, who provided the original opportunity for this project to grow from its inception to completion; and Continuum for providing the means for the glossaries to appear in their various editions.

Aaron The brother of MOSES, chosen by God to be the prophet's spokesperson to the Egyptians. It was Aaron who smote the Red Sea so that it opened and allowed the freed slaves to cross and thus escape the Egyptian forces. It is said that Moses was not able to do this himself as he had once enjoyed the hospitality of Egypt. (*See also* EXODUS)

Ab The categorization of 39 kinds of labour that are forbidden to Jews on the SHABBAT. These are further developed by rabbinical commentators as the categories reflect the period in which they written down in the Scripture – for example, sowing, weaving, planting, building. (*See also* TOLADOT)

Abinu Malkenu A group of 45 supplication prayers recited on specific occasions such as the ten days of penitence, fast days or the Jewish new year.

Abot di Rabbi Nathan A large treatise of Jewish ethics and commentaries that is separate to the MISHNAH and attributed to Rabbi NATHAN.

Abraham The father of the Jewish people who entered the first covenant with God after demonstrating his obedience by offering to sacrifice his son, ISAAC. It is said in the Bible that he was originally a native of the city of Ur in Chaldea but after travelling with his family, he settled near Hebron. Abraham stands as the ideal for the practising Jew who looks to the patriarch to provide the example of faithfulness, longing for the true God and generosity of spirit.

Adonai   *Lit. Lord.* The name most often used to call upon God and used to replace YHVH whenever it appears, as it cannot be pronounced. Adonai reflects the relationship of master and servants but also indicates that the God of Israel is a personal Lord. (*See also* EHYEH ASHER EHYEH)

Afikomen   The portion of MATZAH which is eaten near the end of the SEDER (Passover) and remembers the occasion when the feast ended with eating the paschal lamb sacrificed in the TEMPLE.

Agadah / Aggadah   Part of Jewish oral tradition, contained in the TALMUD, which deals with ethics and moral values based on rabbinical interpretation of the TORAH. The teachings were derived from searching all the books of the Bible for material on ethics, morality, values, theology and history of the Jewish people. The canon of moral and ethical laws that derived from the process of this scriptural interpretation pertained to both the Jewish nation and the individual. The Agadah differs from HALAKHAH in that it provides non-legal material such as folklore, exemplary behaviour of pious Jews, and legends, that can be used to provide examples or support for the laws and regulations. (*See also* MIDRASH)

Agunah   A woman whose husband has disappeared. In ORTHODOX JUDAISM, where there is no evidence of death, the woman is not allowed to remarry. (*See also* HALAKHAH)

Aharonim   *Lit. the later ones.* The Rabbinic authorities who came after the writing down of the SHULHAN ARUKH, the authoritative code of Orthodox Jewish law written in the 16th century CE. Usually these later authorities had to acknowledge the earlier legal decisions of those that came before the writing of the *Shulhan Arukh* as setting the precedent. (*See also* RISHONIM)

Akedah   The story of the 'binding' of ISAAC recounted in Genesis 22 as part of the trials of ABRAHAM. It is read in the SYNAGOGUE during the festival of ROSH HASHANAH.

Al Hanissim   A paragraph inserted into the AMIDAH and the grace recited before meals that proclaims divine deliverance from enemies.

Aleinu / Alenu   An important prayer which comes at the end of all services. The first part proclaims God as the Lord of ISRAEL and the finale looks to the time when all humanity will recognize the glory of God and renounce all idolatry. The prayer was spoken on the occasion of ROSH HASHANAH but is now part of all Jewish liturgy in recognition of its sublime message.

Al-Het   *Lit. for the sin.* A prayer recited at YOM KIPPUR for the pardon of sins.

Aliyah   *Lit. to ascend.* A term used either to refer to the migration of Jews to Israel or to Jews being called to read the SEFER TORAH in the synagogue. Originally every person was called to read but in order not to cause embarrassment for the unlearned, experts in reading Scripture were appointed. The first three readers are traditionally a Cohen, Levi and ISRAEL to represent the historic temple priests, their assistants and the remainder of the tribes of Israel. (*See also* LEVITES)

Almemar   *See* BIMAH.

Amidah   The standing prayer also known as *shemoneh esre*. It is a series of eighteen blessings divided into three parts. The first part consists of three blessings that mention the greatness and goodness of God, His promise to the patriarchs, and His merciful relations with humankind. The middle section consists of twelve blessings, some of which predate the destruction of the TEMPLE. The blessings are mostly concerned with Messianic hopes for the restoration of the lineage of DAVID in a restored JERUSALEM and a return of the scattered Jewish nation to ISRAEL. The final three blessings contain prayers for a life lived in peace and obedience to God's will manifested in the affairs of the daily life. The prayer lies at the heart of Jewish worship and, although the full version is only recited on weekdays, the six benedictions that form the beginning and end are recited at all services.

Amoraim   *Lit. the interpreters.* The term refers to the Talmudic teachers who lived after the editing of the MISHNAH in 200 CE. (*See also* SAVORAIM; TALMUD; TANNAIM)

Amos   One of the books of the Jewish Scriptures that describes the activities and words of the prophet Amos. Amos was a shepherd in the reign of the King Jeroboam II, who was chosen by God to warn the people not to oppress the poor or practise idolatry or live immoral lives. He told the Jewish people that they would be punished harder if they transgressed God's law since they had been chosen to be God's people.

Aninut   The period from death to burial in which the mourner is considered traumatized by the death. It is accepted that the mourner may lose faith in God's justice and therefore he/she should not participate in normal religious activity as it would be hypocritical. Normal occupation should be suspended so that all attention may be given to the funeral arrangements. During this period it is not considered acceptable to give consolation, and the mourner is allowed to be consumed by grief. The funeral itself acts as the catharsis. (*See also* AVELUT; KADDISH; SHELOSHIM; SHIVA)

Apocrypha   Certain works written after the period of the Second TEMPLE which were excluded by the Jews as part of their biblical canon but were added by the Christians to their canon of Scripture, the Old Testament. These include Ecclesiasticus, The Wisdom of Solomon, Macabees I and II, Tobit and Judith. (*See also* TANAKH)

Aqedah   *See* AKEDAH.

Arba Kanfot   A garment worn by Orthodox men and given in childhood, also known as *Tallith Katan*. It is worn underneath one's daily clothing and is a small TALLIT containing the obligatory fringes or ZIZIT.

Arba Kosot   The four cups of wine drunk at the Passover meal or SEDER.

Arba Minim   The festive bouquet of four aromatic plants that have to be ritually arranged as a thanksgiving on the festival of SUKKOT (Harvest). The plants are: i) the branch and fruit of the Citron (*etrog*); ii) the branch of the date palm (LULAV); iii) three branches of the myrtle (*hadassim*); iv) willow branches (*aravot*). The plants symbolize the human society or even the various parts of the single individual. Together they form the whole.

Ark   The original ark was the ARK OF THE COVENANT and the holy ark used in biblical times was used to transport the TORAH. In contemporary Judaism, the ark is a cabinet built into the east wall of a SYNAGOGUE where the scrolls of the Torah are still kept. It is the focal point in the synagogue and its place in the east wall provides the direction of prayer facing towards JERUSALEM. However, if, for some reason, the ark cannot be in the east wall, the congregation will nevertheless face towards the ark. A curtain is usually hung over the front of the ark and some synagogues place two tablets of stone on the outside above the ark to represent the original commandments given to Moses. (*See also* PAROKHET)

Ark of the Covenant   The golden Ark used to transport the two tablets of stone containing the ten commandments given to MOSES.

Aron Hakodesh   *See* ARK.

Ashkenazim   The term used to refer to Jews of Central or East European descent. Originally the term was used for German Jews but today it is commonly used for all Jews of Western as opposed to Eastern descent (SEPHARDIM). The division of Jews into Eastern and Western Jews has existed for at least a thousand years; in ISRAEL, their own Chief Rabbi represents both groups.

Athalta de-geulah   The beginning of the age of redemption that will culminate in the coming of the Messiah. Some Jews believe that this time has already begun, as the return of the promised land of ISRAEL to the Jewish people is a sign of its advent. (*See also* MASSIACH)

Attarah The dark band on the prayer shawl that enables one of the four sides to be differentiated. The band should always be on the outside and on the top when the shawl is worn. (*See also* TALLIT)

Avelut The period of mourning that follows a Jewish funeral. The mourning period is regarded as a time of healing and it follows two stages. The first is SHIVA which lasts for seven days after the burial. After this, there is a further period of 30 days known as SHELOSHIM, but this is extended to one year in the case of the death of a parent. Both periods of mourning are cancelled if a major festival occurs. (*See also* ANINUT; KADDISH; KERIAH)

Avinu Malkinu *Lit. our Father, our King.* A litany that calls on God as Father to reflect the close personal relationship between the Jew and the creator of the universe and also to acknowledge God as ruler and judge of the creation. It is God the King that entered into a covenant with ISRAEL as His chosen and obedient nation. The litany is used in the major Jewish festivals such as YOM KIPPUR and ROSH HASHANAH. (*See also* BERIT)

Avodah The term is taken from the sacrificial rite performed at the TEMPLE by the High Priest on YOM KIPPUR. The instructions for the performance of the original *avodah* are laid out in the Book of LEVITICUS 16, and are still read out in traditional or orthodox synagogues on Yom Kippur. The *avodah* functioned to ritually purify the sanctuary and as an expiation of the people's sins. In the original ceremony a goat was released and sacrificed as a representative of the community's sin. It is this occasion that gave rise to the idea of the 'scapegoat'. The founders of the modern state of ISRAEL used the word *avodah* to mean labour or work in order to indicate that building the new Jewish state was a contemporary form of sacrifice.

Ayn Sof The kabbalistic doctrine of the Godhead, or the idea that behind the successive emanations or SEFIROTH of the divine, there is an absolute, impersonal, incomprehensible being devoid of all qualities known to creation. This being is referred to as *ayin* ('nothingness'). The emanations or *sefiroth* contain the divine qualities such as mercy, compassion and justice. (*See also* KABBALA)

B

Baal Shem Tov *Lit. Master of the Good Name.* The title given to the eighteenth-century mystic and founder of the HASIDIM, born Israel Ben Eleazer in southern Poland. He travelled in Eastern Europe and Russia, where he is believed to have performed many miracles whilst instructing followers in the teachings and practices of KABBALA.

Bar Mitzvah *Lit. son of commandment.* A rite of passage that marks a boy's coming of age at 13 and held on the SHABBAT of the week of his birthday. He is then able to form part of the quorum necessary for the performance of public worship and able to take responsibility for legal decisions. It acknowledges that the boy has reached religious maturity and is no more the responsibility of his father's religious practice but is able to follow God's commandments himself. The boy will be required to read the law at the ceremony in the SYNAGOGUE. The occasion is an important ceremony in contemporary Jewish communities and even non-practising Jews usually observe it. (*See also* BAT MITZVAH)

Bat Mitzvah / Bat Chayil *Lit. daughter of commandment.* The coming-of-age ceremony for girls originally designed by Jacob Ettliner in the nineteenth century, involving a banquet and the recitation of a benediction. The emphasis on this rite of passage will change from community to community but it has become widely accepted in the United States since Mordecai Kaplan devised a SYNAGOGUE ceremony in the early twentieth century. In non-Orthodox communities, the ceremony is virtually identical to the BAR MITZVAH but ORTHODOX synagogues have a more restricted ceremony; however, the girl may be called to read the TORAH at a gathering of women. Outside the United States, the practice is less common in Orthodox communities.

Bedikat Hometz The symbolic search for traces of leavened food that takes place in the home on the night before the occasion of PESACH (Passover). It is symbolic in that leavened food is removed several days before the festival. Traditionally, the head of the household will search with a candle and find a few crumbs that are burnt the following morning. The searching for leavened bread is very popular with children.

Beit ha Knesset Shul *See* BET HA KNESSET.

Berakhah *Lit. blessing.* There are set spoken blessings in Judaism for every aspect of life. These blessings help the practising Jew to develop attunement, a sense of wonder and awe with creation and a never-ending communion with God. (*See also* KAVANAH)

Berit *Lit. covenant.* The reciprocal bond made between God and His chosen people. There are three such covenants made in the Scriptures. The first covenant was made with NOAH after the flood and is binding on all humanity. The second is with ABRAHAM, the first Jew and the father of the people, and for this reason male circumcision is regarded as a covenant. The third covenant was made specifically with the Jewish tribes at Sinai when the law was revealed to MOSES and is eternally binding on all Jews. Jews believe that this covenant makes them God's chosen people with the responsibility to uphold His Will and to love Him. The covenant brings with it reciprocal duties – the Jewish people are God's treasured possession and function as his priests and holy people. This covenant is expressed in the affirmation of the faith or SHEMA taken from DEUTERONOMY 6.5–9 that begins: 'Hear O Israel: the Lord our God, the Lord is One!'. (*See also* BERIT MILAH)

Berit Milah / Brit Milah / Bris *Lit. covenant of circumcision.* All male children are circumcized when they are eight days old. The circumcized male organ is regarded as the seal of the covenant with God, undertaken first by ABRAHAM. Isaac, his second son was circumcized on the eighth day of his life. The preparations for circumcision begin at birth and the main responsibility for the ceremony lies with the father. The parents select two godparents who are honoured with carrying the child to the ceremony and holding him during the act of circumcision. They take on the role of the child's life advisors. The circumcision is performed by a religious specialist known as a MOHEL and the ceremony consists of three parts: *Milah*, the actual cutting of the foreskin from the penis; *P'riah*, another cut that ensures that the remaining skin does not grow back; *Metzitah*, the wiping of the blood. The ceremony is performed in the synagogue or at home. (*See also* BERIT)

Bet Din   *Lit. house of justice.* The traditional court of three RABBIS able to pronounce on matters of Jewish Law. The laws of the court are given in the Book of DEUTERONOMY. Many large Jewish communities have a Bet Din and many Jews would prefer to use its justice rather than go to non-Jewish secular court.

Bet ha Knesset / Beit ha Knesset Shul   *Lit. house of assembly.* An alternative title for the SYNAGOGUE and also the name given to the parliament of the modern state of ISRAEL. (*See also* BET HA TEFILLAH)

Bet ha Midrash   *Lit. house of study.* An alternative name for the SYNAGOGUE. (*See also* BET HA KNESSET; BET HA TEFILLAH)

Bet ha Mikdash   *See* TEMPLE.

Bet ha Tefillah   *Lit. house of prayer.* An alternative name for the SYNAGOGUE. (*See also* BET HA KNESSET; BET HA MIDRASH)

Bible   *See* TANAKH.

Bimah   A raised platform or pulpit in the SYNAGOGUE from which the TORAH is read. It corresponds to the sanctuary in the TEMPLE and contains an eternal flame kept in a simple lamp that symbolizes that the light of the Torah will never die and that the synagogue is always ready to receive worshippers and religious scholars. The pulpit is in the centre of the synagogue so that the people can gather around the Torah.

Binah   One of the ten SEFIROTH or emanations of the AYN SOF or Godhead. *Binah* refers to the spelling out of the details of creation in the divine mind (*See also* KABBALA).

Birkat ha-Mozon   The four benedictions recited as a grace after meals. The first benediction is an expression of gratitude to God for providing the food; the second thanks God for giving the TORAH and the promised land; the third is a prayer of redemption and a request for the return of JERUSALEM; and the last is a prayer of general thanksgiving.

Bris   *See* BERIT MILAH.

Brit Milah   *See* BERIT MILAH.

C

Cabala   *See* KABBALA.

Capel   *See* KIPPAH.

Caro, Joseph   (1488–1575). A famous RABBI and mystic who wrote the SHULHAN ARUKH, the definitive codification used by traditional Jews in order to interpret the laws of the TORAH and maintain Jewish life.

Challah   *See* HALLAH.

Chanukiah   *See* MENORAH.

Chanukkah   *See* HANUKKAH.

Chasidim   *See* HASIDIM.

Chazen   *See* HAZZAN.

Chronicles   The two books of Chronicles are counted as one work and together comprise one of the twelve books of the Hebrew Scriptures that are known as Holy Writings. It consists of a survey of biblical history, but particularly focuses on the role of the priesthood and the forms of worship in the TEMPLE at JERUSALEM. (*See also* KETUVIM; TANAKH)

Chuppah   *See* HUPPAH.

D

Daniel   A book of the Scriptures that describes a time when Judaism was in danger of extinction after conquest and persecution by the Greeks under Antiochus. The book describes the persecution of the prophet Daniel and the divine intervention that saved him during the earlier period of conquest and slavery under the Persians. It thus provides an example of courage, forbearance and faithfulness in the new apparently hopeless situation.

Dat   The Hebrew word used to express religion. It meaning is nearer to law rather than to express belief.

Dati   A term used in ISRAEL to describe militant or traditionalist adherents to Judaism.

David   The King of ISRAEL after SAUL who united the two kingdoms of Judah and Ephraim and established his capital at JERUSALEM. David was believed to have been 'anointed' or chosen by God and various scriptural verses state the descendents of David will rule over the kingdom of Israel for ever. After the division of the land and its subsequent defeat and conquest by the Greeks and the Romans, the belief in a messiah from the house of David became a part of Jewish tradition. David is also believed to be the originator of the physical format of the Jewish prayer. (*See also* MASSIACH)

Dayyan   A RABBI who acts as a judge in a religious court to make decisions on matters of Jewish religious law. The ultimate judge is

God. (*See also* BET DIN; HALAKHAH)

Deborah   A woman who achieves the status of a judge and who goes to war as a leader as described in the Book of JUDGES.

Derek Eretz   A term used for good manners but also the title of a book on ethics and right conduct.

Deuteronomy   The fifth book of the SEFER TORAH which contains the words of MOSES and the Book of the Covenant. (*See also* BERIT; PENTATEUCH; TORAH)

Devekut   The intimate, one-pointed enduring contemplation of God that is the goal of the mystic's endeavour as described in KABBALA.

Diaspora   The term used to describe the dispersion of the Jewish people throughout the world after the fall of JERUSALEM and the destruction of the TEMPLE in 70 CE. The Jewish people have suffered various exiles and they are all associated with the loss of the promised land or ISRAEL. Exile has become associated with Messianic expectations in Jewish belief where the return of the people to the Promised Land would occur simultaneously with the coming of the Messiah. (*See also* MASSIACH)

Din   The act of justice or a judgement made on a specific law in the religious court. It can also be used to describe the law in general. (*See also* BET DIN; DAYYAN; HALAKHAH)

E

Ecclesiastes   A book included in the Hebrew Scriptures after many years of debate. It contains the words of Solomon and teaches the ultimate vanity of all worldly activities. The debate amongst RABBIS was not concerned with its message but as to whether the words were inspired by God or simply SOLOMON's own sayings. (*See also* APOCRYPHA; TANAKH)

Ehyeh Asher Ehyeh   *Lit. I am who I am*. The description that God provided for Himself when MOSES asked for a name that he could reveal to the people. In ancient cultures, knowledge of a name was often perceived to provide power over the name's owner. God's refusal to give His name indicates that the Jewish people could have no power over Him, as His power was eternal and unlimited. God's name is regarded as ineffable and may not be pronounced. It consists of the unpronounceable letters YHVH rendered as Jehovah. (*See also* ADONAI)

Ein Keloheinu   *Lit. There is nobody like our God*. A hymn sung towards the culmination of morning services in the SYNAGOGUE. In ASHKENAZI synagogues it is only sung on the Sabbath or festival days.

El   Hebrew for 'God' and one of the biblical names of God used instead of the unspoken YHVH.

Elijah   The prophet who is believed to come again as a forerunner to the Messiah. He is regarded as the guardian of ISRAEL and according to the Scriptures never died, as he was taken up to heaven in a fiery chariot (II Kings 2.11–12). It is believed that he will return at the end of time to tell the world that the Messiah is here. As the protector of Israel and the covenant, his name is invoked on important religious occasions such as the Passover and circumcision. He is also called upon to protect Jews in the coming week at the finale of the Sabbath. (*See also* BERIT MILAH; MASSIACH; PESACH; SHABBAT)

El male rahamim   *Lit. God full of compassion.* A prayer for the souls of the dead recited at funerals and memorial services.

Ellul   The Jewish month that runs from August to September that is used as a month of preparation for some of the most important religious occasions in the Jewish calendar known as the Days of Awe. (*See also* ROSH HASHANAH; YOM KIPPUR)

Elohim   Hebrew for 'God(s)' and one of the biblical names of God used instead of the unspoken YHVH.

Emunah   *Lit. faith.* The foundation of the Jewish tradition, it essentially refers to trust in God and reliance on Him to guide the people perfectly. If a person trusts completely in God, everything else will fall into place.

Erev Shabbat   Friday, the eve of the Sabbath, which is used to prepare for the holiest day of the week. On this day, Jews should try to create an atmosphere of holiness that will prepare them for the day of rest that follows. The Sabbath food is prepared, the family dress for the occasion and the table is set. Traditionally, the Sabbath is said to begin when the mother lights the two candles on the table and gives the blessing. In the SYNAGOGUE, the Sabbath is welcomed and the congregation recites PSALMS 95–9. They then face towards the door of the synagogue to welcome the Sabbath whilst singing a hymn composed by Rabbi Solomon Halevi Alkabetz (sixteenth century). Afterwards, normal prayer resumes but the worship ends with the KIDDUSH and wine. The congregation depart for their homes after greeting each other with 'Shabbat Shalom'. Once home, the father will bless his wife and then the parents bless their children, after which the Sabbath meal is taken. The father recites the Kiddush and speaks of the GENESIS verses in which God sanctifies time by appointing the Sabbath as holy. Each member of the family will partake of the wine from the Kiddush cup. A blessing is spoken over the HALLAH bread, which is then partaken by each member of the family. Grace and the reading of Psalm 126 complete the celebration. (*See also* SHABBAT)

Erub   A device that was used in traditional Jewish communities to mitigate the severity of the Sabbath codes regarding the carrying of objects. A section of the streets in a town was separated off by fixing a wire supported by two poles. The street was then considered to be fenced off and its status changed from public to private property. No longer regarded as a public thoroughfare, it became a place where people were allowed then to carry objects. (*See also* ERUB TEHUHIM; SHABBAT)

Erub Tehuhim   A device to mitigate the severity of the Sabbath laws regarding the distance that a person is permitted to walk. It is stated in the Scriptures that one should not leave his/her 'place' on the Sabbath. Oral law interprets place as the distance of 2,000 cubits (just over half a mile) on either side of the town of residence in which one can walk purely for pleasure. (*See also* ERUB; SHABBAT)

Esau   The son of ISAAC and twin brother of JACOB who loses his birthright on the death of his father after being tricked by their mother, as recounted in GENESIS.

Esther   The ward of a Jewish sage named Mordecai, whose legendary story is told in the Book of Esther in the Scriptures. She was chosen to be the new bride of the Persian King Ahasverus, who did not know that she was a Jew. Her father saved the king's life by revealing to his daughter a palace plot. Later, the king appointed a new viceroy, who was enraged by Mordecai's refusal to bow to him and therefore plotted to have all the Jews killed. Esther intervened to save her people and bring down the viceroy who was hanged on the gallows that he had built for Mordecai. Her father was appointed viceroy is his place. The story is used as an early example of anti-Semitism, as the Book of Esther elaborates on the reasons cited by the viceroy to persuade the king that the Jews should be destroyed. They eerily echo the reasons that have been used for the persecution of the Jews throughout their history in DIASPORA. The story of Esther is celebrated in the Feast of PURIM.

Etrog   A fruit, similar to a lemon, used in the ritual of the festival of SUKKOT. (*See also* ARBA MINIM)

Exodus   The second book of the SEFER TORAH which contains the account of the liberation of the Israelites from slavery in Egypt and the revelation of the TORAH to MOSES on Mount Sinai. The Passover festival traditionally celebrates the occasion when Moses led his people to freedom. (*See also* PENTATEUCH; PESACH)

Ezekial   A prophet with a book of the Scriptures named after him. He rebuked the people for accepting the Egyptian practice of worshipping the sun. The source of the Jewish prayer for the dead can be found in the Book of Ezekial. (*See also* KADDISH)

Ezra   Ezra was a scribe who led a group of Jews back from exile in Babylon. There is a book of the Hebrew Scriptures named after him in the section known as Holy Writings. Ezra is believed to have been a religious leader of the Jewish people soon after their release from captivity by the Babylonians in the sixth century BCE. Ezra led a religious revival and restored the TORAH to its place of prominence in Jewish life. It is believed that he instituted the reading of the Torah on the afternoon of the SHABBAT. (*See also* KETUVIM; NEHEMIAH; TANAKH)

G

Gabbai   The treasurer or warden of a SYNAGOGUE.

Galut   *See* DIASPORA.

Gaon   *Lit. excellency.* The title given to the head of one of the Talmudic academies in Iraq during the Geonic period from the mid-sixth century to the mid-eleventh century CE.

Gehenna / Gehinnon   The place of burning or torment which is the equivalent of hell as described in Jewish apocryphal literature. It is not regarded as eternal punishment but a place where the wicked are punished until the Day of Resurrection, when all will be judged. Not all Jews share the same beliefs regarding hell and punishment, and many have interpreted hell as a figurative state of existence in which the soul is separated from God.

Gemara / Gemarah   *Lit. completion.* The commentary on the MISHNAH contained in the TALMUD in which the AMORAIM (early rabbinical scholars) expound and develop the oral law in order to reach an accurate interpretation of a scriptural command. The commentary is written in Aramaic and deals primarily with festivals, ceremonies, legal matters, social conduct and education.

Gematria   The art of using numerology to search for links between the names of God and the words of the Bible, possibly introduced by the mystic Abu Aaron in the ninth century. It has become part of the KABBALA tradition.

Genesis The first of the five books of the Hebrew Scriptures that form the PENTATEUCH, the heart of the TORAH. The book describes the creation of the world and the human race and gives an account of the relationship between God and NOAH, ABRAHAM, ISAAC and JACOB, the patriarchs of the Jewish people. The final chapters tell the story of Joseph and his rise to power in Egypt. (*See also* PENTATEUCH; TORAH)

Genizah A storage place in the SYNAGOGUE used for damaged religious texts or for the disposal of worn-out texts, usually by burial.

Geonim The heads of the important Talmudic academies of the Middle East responsible for developing the teachings of the TALMUD and spreading them throughout the Jewish world. They were particularly skilled in codifying Jewish law and developed RESPONSA literature in which queries were addressed through the format of questions and answers. The period of the *Geonim* is known as the Gaonic and it ended in the eleventh century CE when the centre of scholarship shifted to Spain and North Africa. (*See also* SAVORAIM; SHEELOT U-TESHUVOT)

Ger A Jewish proselyte. Conversion into Judaism has always been allowed but has passed through several stages. Up until the period of the Roman Empire, conversion was encouraged and the new convert entered fully into Jewish life and received a new name. During the period of the Roman Empire, Jewish missionary activity was widespread but when Christianity became the state religion of the Empire, conversion to Judaism was punishable by death. This may have led to the Orthodox reluctance about conversion that exists in the present. During the period of the Second TEMPLE it was established that the convert should be motivated only by religious conviction, but today converts are accepted on the grounds of mixed marriage. A long period of instruction is required in Orthodoxy but the Reform tradition makes conversion easier.

Gershom, Rabbi (940–1028) Known as the 'Light of the Exile' and a famous writer of 'responsa literature', which is a series of questions and answers dealing with queries on matters of Jewish law. He issued a decree banning polygamy in 1000. Originally followed only by the ASHKENAZI nations, this is now followed by all Jews throughout the world. He also stated that a woman could not be divorced against her will.

Gersonides (1288–1344) A Jewish philosopher and writer of scriptural commentary. The medieval period saw a flowering of Jewish philosophy as they came to grips with Aristotle and Plato. Gersonides moved more towards neo-Platonism. (*See also* MAIMONIDES)

Get A bill of divorce issued by a Jewish court that can dissolve the KETUBAH (marriage contract). The *get* must be accepted freely by all parties and each one is written individually and signed by two witnesses. It has thirteen lines and must be written without any errors or corrections. The *get* is placed into the hands of the woman, who is then divorced. She returns it to the presiding RABBI who files it and after 92 days she is free to remarry. A man who remarries without a *get* is considered to have committed polygamy; a woman commits adultery.

Gevurah *Lit. power.* One of the ten SEFIROTH or emanations of the AYN SOF that represent the aspects of God working in creation. *Gevurah* is the power or judgement that prevents the love of God (HESED) overwhelming all creatures and instilling in them a longing to merge back into Him. A balance of power and love is required for the world to exist. (*See also* KABBALA)

Gog and Magog Two names mentioned in the apocalyptic vision decribed by Ezekial in Ezekial 38.9. The prophet speaks of a war between the Lord and Gog of the land of Magog. Traditional Jewish rabbinical sources state the war with Gog and Magog will precede the coming of the Messiah. (*See also* MASSIACH)

Golah   *See* DIASPORA.

Golem   A legendary monster created out of clay by the Maharal of Prague, a kabbalist. Given life by means of the magical use of the names of God, it was created to protect the Jews of Prague against persecution. (*See also* KABBALA)

Gomel   *Lit. bountiful.* A blessing given in the SYNAGOGUE to celebrate deliverance from danger.

Goy   A derogatory term used for a non-Jew.

H

Habukkuk A prophet and a book of the same name that is included in the Jewish Scriptures. Habbukuk was probably a contemporary of JEREMIAH. The book is concerned with the question of divine justice, and the prophet asks why a non-believing nation such as the Chaldeans should be chosen to carry out God's punishment of the tribes of Israel, as they will kill both the just and the wicked. (*See also* NEVIIM; TANAKH)

Haftarah A passage from one of the books of the Prophets read in the SYNAGOGUE either on the Sabbath or at the major festivals. It is used as a supplement to the TORAH reading but is selected to coincide with the message contained in the Torah scrolls on that day's reading. The reading takes place prior to the reading from the SEFER TORAH. (*See also* NEVIIM; TANAKH)

Hag The term for a Jewish festival, as in *Hag ha-Katsir*, the Feast of the Harvest, or Hag *Ha'aviv*, the Holiday of the Spring, alternative names for SHAVUOT or PESACH.

Hag Sameah *Lit. happy festival*. The traditional Hebrew greeting used by Jews on festival days.

Hagadah / Haggadah *Lit. telling*. The prayer book used on the eve of the Passover for the SEDER ritual that contains the narrative or storytelling that goes with the meal. The *New Hagadah* was produced in 1942 and contains references to the plight of the Jews in Nazi Germany. (*See also* PESACH)

Haggai   A prophet and a book of the same name included in the Jewish Scriptures. He began his mission in 520 BCE amongst the returned exiles who had been released by Cyrus in 538 BCE. Haggai encouraged the returning Jews to begin building the Second TEMPLE in spite of opposition from the Samaritans. (*See also* NEVIIM; TANAKH)

Hagiographa   The third of the three Jewish divisions of Scripture, variously arranged, but usually comprising the PSALMS, PROVERBS, JOB, Song of SOLOMON, RUTH, LAMENTATIONS, ECCLESIASTES, ESTHER, DANIEL, EZRA, NEHEMIAH and CHRONICLES. Also called the Writings. (*See also* TANAKH)

Haham   *Lit. sage.* The honorific title used to address a Sephardic RABBI. (*See also* SEPHARDIM)

Halakhah / Halacha   Jewish law as contained in the TALMUD, comprising of rabbinical debates and discussions on rules and regulations derived from interpretation of the TORAH. It is used as a guide for every aspect of life. (*See also* AGGADAH)

Hallah / Challah   The two loaves of white bread used during festivals and on the Sabbath, over which the blessings and the grace before meals are recited. The loaves are covered with a cloth and symbolize the manna on which the Jews miraculously survived whilst wandering in the wilderness after their release from Egypt. It is said in the Book of EXODUS that the manna fell in a double portion before the Sabbath. (*See also* SEDER; SHABBAT)

Hallaph   The knife used in the ritual slaughter of animals and poultry for meat. (*See also* KASHRUT; SHECHITA; SHOHET)

Hallel   The repetition of Psalms 113–18 that takes place in the Morning Prayer liturgy on special occasions, such as the three festivals, but is forbidden on the high holy days of Yom Kippur and Rosh Hashanah. (*See also* PESACH; SHAVUOT; SUKKOT; TEFILLAH)

Hamets   Yeast or leaven normally used to bake bread but forbidden in Jewish homes during the festival of Passover. (*See also* SEDER)

Hanukiah   *See* MENORAH.

Hanukkah / Chanukkah   The Feast of Dedication also known as the Feast of Lights, from the use of the MENORAH during the eight days of the festival. It is celebrated in the month of Kislev (5 November – 3 December). On the first day, one branch of the candle is lit, a process repeated each day until finally the whole candelabra is lit. It commemorates the victory of Judas Maccabaeus over Antiochus V Epiphanes which led to the rededication of the TEMPLE in JERUSALEM in 165 BCE. The festival is a minor one in the Jewish religious year as the winter festivals are considered to be man-made, unlike the summer festivals, which are divine ordinances in the TORAH; despite this, however, it has become very popular.

Haredi   An adherent of traditional Judaism.

Haroset   One of the foods partaken of in the ritual meal at the Passover. It consists of a mixture of apples, nuts, cinnamon and sometimes a little wine blended into a creamy sauce. (*See also* PESACH; SEDER)

Ha-Shem   *Lit. the Name.* One of the scriptural names of God used instead of the unspoken YHVH.

Hashgahah   A central belief in Judaism that God is the controller and guide of the entire universe. All events are therefore ultimately pre-ordained and there is a good providence operating everywhere throughout the creation. This benevolent providence operates both generally throughout creation and in special events that take place in the life of an individual. It is believed that nothing takes place by accident.

Hasidim / Chasidim   A religious movement founded by Rabbi Israel ben Eliezer (1700–60), better known as the BAAL SHEM TOV, in the middle of the eighteenth century in Eastern Europe. The movement rapidly gained popularity and won thousands of members throughout Poland, Russia, Lithuania, Hungary and Romania. It stressed piety and joyful worship over the intellectual study of the TALMUD. There are two basic beliefs that make Hasidism unique. The first is the idea of DEVEKUT or attachment to God. For the Hasidim all things are pervaded by God and the only true reality is God, therefore God should be remembered in everything that we do. Consequently, the Hasidim should always be filled with the joy of God's presence (*simhah*) and be humble before that presence (*shiflut*). Those that achieve this state of *devekut, simhah* and *shiflut* are regarded as holy men fit to teach or lead others. This resulted in a new kind of REBBE or leader who attracted disciples as opposed to the traditional rabbis who were versed in law. In time, dynasties developed from the various great rebbes and formed religious subgroups within the movement such as the Lubavitch, Sotmar, Ger, Beltz and Vishnitz. The Hasidim are also distinctive in their dress. They wear a long cloak (*kapote*), a fur hat made of sable with thirteen tails (*streimel*) and a special belt when in prayer (*gartle*). They are also recognizable from their long curled beards. Hasidic prayer is accompanied by melody and from time to time individuals will break out into ecstatic dance in which one leg is always kept off the ground. (*See also* ZADDIKIM)

Haskalah   *Lit. enlightenment.* Usually used to describe the eighteenth-century movement led by Moses Mendelssohn which emphasized education and the study of Scripture within a modern framework. Mendelssohn translated the PENTATEUCH into German so that it would become available to Jews in their own spoken language. The movement encouraged Jews to abandon medieval ways of life and thought. It spread from Prussia to Austria and then into Russia. (*See also* REFORM JUDAISM)

Hatan Torah   *Lit. the groom of the Torah.* The last reader of the Torah on the joyful celebration of SIMHAT TORAH. He is called to read the final portion of the Torah for the culmination of the religious year. He will walk to the BIMAH escorted by children. It is deemed a special privilege and usually reserved for an elder person known for their piety and goodness.

Hatimah   *Lit. sealing.* A liturgical formula used at the culmination of a blessing.

Hatimah Tovah   A greeting used at YOM KIPPUR meaning 'May your entry in the heavenly book of life be sealed for good in the coming year'.

Hatturat Horaah   *Lit: permission to lay down a decision.* The formal permission to make decisions concerning matters of law and ritual conferred on a newly qualified RABBI. Nowadays, new rabbis are provided with a certificate which includes the phrase '*yoreh yoreh, yadin yadin*' (He may surely give a decision and may surely judge). (*See also* KETAV SEMIKHAH; SEMIKHAH; YESHIVA)

Havdalah   The service at the end of the Sabbath which is celebrated at home and in the SYNAGOGUE. It requires a KIDDUSH cup, a plate on which the cup is set, a spice box filled with sweet-smelling spices and a twisted candle. The wine is blessed and the spice box is passed round for everyone to smell as a symbol of the last fragrance of the Sabbath. The candle is then lifted up whilst a blessing is recited. The leader drinks the wine and then passes it around to the members partaking in the ceremony. The candle is traditionally extinguished by the wine that has overflowed onto the plate to mark the end of the Sabbath. (*See also* SHABBAT)

Hazanut / Chazanut   The art of singing or chanting Scripture in the correct manner in the services held in the SYNAGOGUE. This is the responsibility of the cantor, who learns and performs the required melodies ands cadences. (*See also* HAZZAN)

Hazzan / Chazan   The cantor who leads the congregation in the singing and chanting of Scripture and prayer in the services of the SYNAGOGUE. In early Jewish literature the cantor is known as 'the deputy of the congregation', reflecting the fact that he is the one chosen to speak to God on behalf of the congregation. In the SHULHAN ARUKH, it is written that the cantor must have the following qualifications: a good voice, an impeccable character, and be accepted to the congregation. (*See also* HAZANUT)

Hebrew *See* IVRIT.

Hesed *Lit. loving kindness.* According to the tradition of the KABBALA, the fifth of the ten SEFIROTH who emanate from the AYN SOF. Second on the right-hand branch of the Tree of Life underneath *Hokhmah*, it is the love that God has for His creatures and is controlled by the GEVURAH, the power of discrimination or judgement.

Heter Permission to teach signifying the ordination of a RABBI.

Hevrah Kabranim The traditional organization that existed in every Jewish community and received the bodies of dead Jews at the graveyard. They were responsible for the digging of the grave, the placing of the body in the grave and the final filling in with soil. In the past, it was traditional that all funeral services were not paid for. (*See also* HEVRAH KADISHAH)

Hevrah Kadishah The traditional organization that existed in every Jewish community to provide the services required for the dead. The members of the organization would be called to sit with the dying person throughout the day and night, making sure that they confessed and uttered the SHEMA on their dying breath. After death had been confirmed, they took the body away to be prepared for the funeral. They washed and dressed the deceased, prepared the coffin and took the body to the cemetery, where it became the responsibility of the gravediggers. (*See also* HEVRAH KABRANIM; TAHARAH; TUMAH)

Hibbat Zion An early form of ZIONISM which begun in nineteenth-century Eastern Europe.

Hiddur Mitzvah The manifestation of zeal or rectitude in obedience to religious observances.

Hillel, Rabbi A famous first-century CE RABBI who founded the School of Hillel. There is a well-known story that he was asked by a would-be convert to teach him the TORAH in the period that he could stand on one leg. It is said that Hillel replied, 'Do unto others as you would be done by.' He claimed that this was the essence of the Torah and all the rest was commentary. This is known as the 'golden rule'.

Hilloni　A term used for a Jew who does not follow the religion. A secular Jew.

Hillul ha-shem　An action performed by a Jew that brings disgrace or disrepute on the Jewish community and therefore shames God.

Hod　*Lit. splendour.* According to the tradition of the KABBALA, it is the seventh of the ten SEFIROTH who emanate from the AYN SOF. It is the third on the left-hand side of the Tree of Life and, along with NETZAH, is one of the two supports for the *sefiroth*.

Hokhmah　*Lit. wisdom.* According to the tradition of the KABBALA, it is the third of the ten SEFIROTH who emanate from the AYN SOF. It is the first on the right-hand side of the Tree of Life, and is the 'point', the first flash of an idea in which the whole of creation is spelled out in the divine mind.

Hol ha-Moed　The intermediate days of the festivals of PESACH and SUKKOT that are distinguished from the named sacred days and are observed as semi-holy days. Essential work is allowed and in the SYNAGOGUE, HALLEL and MUSSAF are read in addition to the TORAH. (*See also* HOSHANA RABBA)

Hosea　A prophet and a book of the same name included in the Jewish Scriptures. Hosea was a contemporary of ISAIAH. He warned against the evil doing and injustice that he saw in the reign of Jeroboam II in the middle of the eighth century BCE. Speaking of the relationship between God and His chosen people in terms of the intimate relationship between a husband and a wife, he preaches that if only the unfaithful wife would repent her sins, then the faithful husband would forgive her. (*See also* NEVIIM; TANAKH)

Hoshana   A prayer for salvation recited in the SYNAGOGUE during the festival of SUKKOT.

Hoshana Rabba   The last of the intermediate days of the festival of SUKKOT that falls on the seventh day. In the time of the TEMPLE it used to be known as the 'day of the willow branch' after the custom of the priests to circle the altar seven times beating the floor with willow branches. Today, seven circuits are made around the TORAH scrolls whist reciting Hoshana prayers. In the past, the day was also associated with prayers for rain but it is now regarded as the day when divine judgement will be handed out. Pious Jews will pass the night in the SYNAGOGUE reading the Torah. The association with judgement makes the day a solemn occasion. (*See also* HOL HA-MOED)

Huldah   A prophetess and an example of a pious woman, who lived in JERUSALEM and was sought out by the leaders of the people after the discovery of the TORAH in the damaged TEMPLE. She advised the King of Judah to continue in obedience and humility (II Kings 22.14–20).

Humash   A single volume that contains only the five books of the TORAH.

Huppah / Chuppah   The canopy that forms a sacred space under which the bride and groom stand surrounded by both parents and the RABBI during a Jewish wedding. The basic form of the *huppah* is a canopy supported on four poles. Some are very simple but others are highly decorated. (*See also* KIDDUSHIN; NISUIN)

Hurban   *Lit. destruction.* A term derived from the destruction of the First and Second TEMPLES in JERUSALEM, often used for the genocide of Jews in Europe by the Nazis.

Isaac   One of the first Jewish patriarchs and the son of ABRAHAM who, according to the Hebrew Scriptures was offered to God in sacrifice as a test of his father's submission. Isaac is seen as the ideal of Judaism, in that he was willing to offer himself as a sacrifice. The binding of Isaac (AKEDAH), as described in GENESIS 22.1–15, is celebrated by Jews on the eve of the feast of ROSH HASHANAH.

Isaiah   One of the most important prophets and a book of the same name in the Hebrew Scriptures. He may have been a member of the royal family and prophesied during the reigns of Jotham, Ahaz and Hezekiah. It is believed by the scriptural authorities in Judaism that the utterances of Isaiah were written down and edited by Hezekiah and his scribes. Isaiah's prophecies outspokenly criticize the people for their religious hypocrisy, poor moral standards, oppression of the poor and corruption amongst their leaders. He warns of divine punishment but indicates that a remnant of the people will uphold the truth. (*See also* NEVIIM)

Israel / Yisrael   *Lit. one who struggles with God.* It refers to the worldwide community of Jews or the land of Israel. It is also the name of the modern Jewish state founded in 1948. The worldwide community of Jews represents the totality of ISRAEL, and it is to this people that the TORAH, or law of God, was given in the covenant accepted by MOSES and the Jewish people. The land of Israel was promised to Moses and his people and is regarded as the Holy Land. The site of the TEMPLE, it is the land where all the prophets and patriarchs lived and taught, and the location of JERUSALEM. Whenever the Jewish people have lost the land through conquest or invasion, they have regarded themselves as exiles and developed religious traditions and practices to maintain the ideal of Israel in their hearts and minds. They have always prayed for a return to the land and the messianic ideal of Judaism is bound up with the return of Israel. Even after the destruction of the Second Temple by the Romans and the consequent dispersion of the people, some Jews remained in Jerusalem, and the city of Safat in Galilee was a great centre of KABBALA. During the persecution of Jews in Eastern Europe and Germany, the desire for the return of Israel was campaigned for by the Zionist movement and finally achieved. The return of the Holy land to the Jews has been a source of conflict with the Muslim world ever since and is further complicated by the fact that Jerusalem is holy to three world religions: Judaism, Christianity and Islam. There are also tensions within the Jewish community amongst the Orthodox movements as many of them do not accept the idea of a modern secular state of Israel but look to a return of the religious state and the coming of the Messiah. (*See also* BERIT; MASSIACH; ZIONISM)

Isru Chag   *Lit. to bind the festival.* The day that follows directly after the feasts of PESACH, SHAVUOT, and SUKKOT.

Ivrit   The Hebrew language in which the Scriptures are written. It is used in the Orthodox SYNAGOGUE services and Jewish prayer. Traditionally, young Jews would study Hebrew in order to know their religion. While the language has been restored to everyday use in ISRAEL, many religious Jews will still only use it for sacred purposes.

J

Jacob   One of the first Jewish patriarchs; the son of ISAAC and the father of JONAH who had been forced to flee from his brother ESAU. Jacob represents the balance between mercy and judgement.

Jeremiah   An important prophet and book of the same name in the Hebrew Scriptures. He was born near Jerusalem and prophesied in the reign of King Josiah until after the Assyrians arrived in 586 BCE and the destruction of the First TEMPLE in JERUSALEM. He was frequently imprisoned for condemning the priests for idolatry and hypocrisy. He prophesied for over forty years and his utterances were maintained by his scribe, Baruch. (*See also* NEVIIM)

Jerusalem   Jerusalem or Yerusalem is the geographical focus of the Jewish people, expressed in one of the PSALMS of DAVID as 'if I forget thee, O Jerusalem may my right hand lose its cunning' (137.5). Jews pray facing in the direction of the city and ask God to rebuild it in its ancient glory as in the time of DAVID and SOLOMON. A similar prayer is recited after every meal, and YOM KIPPUR and PESACH have long been celebrated in DIASPORA by the climax of 'next year Yerusalem'.

Jethro   The father-in-law of MOSES and priest of Midian with whom Moses stayed whilst hiding in exile from Egypt after killing an Egyptian officer who was mistreating some Jewish slaves.

Jew   *See* YEHUDIM.

Job   A righteous man who suffered badly and questioned God as to the reason why. The problems of Job provide a dialogue to consider the human situation and suffering. The conclusion is that a human being must have complete faith in God and endure everything patiently. One of the books of the Hebrew Scriptures is named after him and focuses on his trials. Some Jewish commentators have suggested that the Book of Job was written by Moses. The book is included in the part of the Bible known as Holy Writings. (*See also* EMUNAH; KETUVIM)

Joel   One of the twelve minor prophets and a short book of the same name in the Hebrew Scriptures, although the twelve books are treated as one because of their brevity. It is not known when Joel prophesied: some argue that he is one of the oldest prophets, whilst others state that he is associated with the return from exile in Assyria. Joel called upon the nation of ISRAEL to repent their sins and turn to God, and he is famous for prophesying the destruction of Judah by a plague of locusts. (*See also* NEVIIM)

Jonah   One of the twelve minor prophets and a short book of the same name in the Hebrew Scriptures, although the twelve books are treated as one because of their brevity. It is not known when the prophet lived but some Jewish commentators have identified him with Jonah, the son of Amittai, who prophesied in the reign of King Jeroboam II. Although Jonah's story of his flight from God after being called to bring the people of Ninevah to righteousness and his subsequent sojourn in the belly of a whale is well known, he is regarded in Judaism as the epitome of the futility of humans trying to escape their obligations to the creator. (*See also* NEVIIM)

Joshua   A leader of the people of Israel and a book of the Hebrew Scriptures included amongst the early prophets. Joshua led the people in the conquest of the land of Canaan after the death of MOSES. It is Joshua who leads the people across the banks of the River Jordan into the Promised Land of ISRAEL. The Book of Joshua tells of the miraculous events at the fall of the city of Jericho when the sun stood still in the sky and the walls of the city fell to allow the armies of Joshua to be victorious.

Judah ha-Nasi   A second-century CE Palestinian RABBI, otherwise known as Judah the Prince, whose great achievement was to arrange the material of the TALMUD into a concise, clearly arranged text covering the whole of Jewish life known as the MISHNAH. This work was essential after the destruction of the Second TEMPLE in 70 CE by the Romans and the dispersion of the Jewish people from the land of ISRAEL.

Judaism   *See* YAHADUT.

Judges   One of the books of the Hebrew Scriptures included in the section known as the Prophets. The Book of Judges is regarded as belonging to the early period of prophecy. The lives of the prophets SAMUEL, NATHAN, ELIJAH and Elisha are introduced, but the teachings focus on the issue of kingship and obedience to God. The judges were inspired leaders of the nation who were chosen for their qualities of justice, selflessness and heroism to liberate the people of ISRAEL from their enemies. They included DEBORAH, Gideon and SAMSON. (*See also* NEVIIM)

K

Kabbala / Kabbalah / Cabala Jewish mystics have long believed that it is possible to have so close an intimacy or relationship with God, that His presence can be seen with the eye of the Spirit. Studies that penetrated the TORAH in the light of such wisdom were carried out by Jewish sages. Such figures occur in the TALMUD but ORTHODOX JUDAISM always had a tense relationship with these mystical teachings, which were on one hand respected but on the other seen to be fraught with danger. A vast literature known as *Hekhalot* refers to the heavenly halls or stages through which the mystic travels on the inner journey of the soul. In the twelfth century CE, there was an increase in Jewish mysticism, which drew upon these ancient traditions but began to develop a systematic and coherent theosophy that is now known as Kabbala. The tradition is passed down from master to disciple, and the corpus of work known as the ZOHAR contains the kabbalistic interpretation of the five books of MOSES. The city of Safat in the Galilee became the great centre for the Study of Kabbala and was famous for the piety and devotion of its mystical RABBIS. They practised their mystical disciplines, led ascetic existences, studied the Torah unceasingly, gave to charity and maintained strict control over their mental and emotional moods to avoid lust or anger. This simple mysticism based on the love of God and the longing to seek closeness with Him has been complicated by arcane studies of numerology and sometimes far-fetched secret interpretations of Torah. (*See also* AYN SOF; SEFIROTH)

Kaddish   A very special prayer recited in Aramaic that expresses the hope of eternal peace in God and affirms God's holiness. It was written in Aramaic as that was the language used by Jews after the Babylonian exile. The prayer is used in the SYNAGOGUE to mark the completion of a section of the service such as the AMIDAH or the culmination of the service but the most famous Kaddish is the mourner's prayer recited for eleven months after the death of a parent (although it can be used for other close relatives). The Kaddish is also recited after completion of a period of study of the TORAH. (*See also* SHELOSHIM)

Kadosh   *Lit. set apart.* The idea that the Jew sets him/herself apart from the world in order to join with God. It would be expressed through maintenance of the laws and commandments and the concept of a chosen people. (*See also* BERIT; KAVANAH)

Kadosh Barukh Hu   *Lit. Holy One Blessed is He.* One of the names of God used instead of the unspoken YHVH.

Kapparot   A custom practised only by some Orthodox Jewish communities and regarded as superstition by many RABBIS. It is based on the ancient idea of ransom, in which one life can be sacrificed to preserve another. A cockerel is selected for a male and a hen for a female; it is taken by the head of the household to a group of men and whirled three times around the heads of the group. Sacred words are recited requesting that the life of the bird should be taken as a ransom for the life of the person. The bird is then killed. It is essential that this act should not be confused with the sacrifice at the TEMPLE, which ceased after the expulsion of the Jews from ISRAEL in 70 CE when the Temple was destroyed.

Kasher   *See* KOSHER.

Kashrut   The term that is used to denote Jewish dietary laws worked out by rabbinical interpretation of the food restrictions implied by the ordinances in the TORAH. The Scriptures forbid eating any four-footed, cloven-hooved animal that does not chew the cud, fish that do not have fins and scales and all birds of prey and members of the crow family. Insects, reptiles and shellfish are also forbidden, along with any animal that has not been killed according to the Jewish rules of slaughter and drained of blood, or found to be diseased after correct slaughter. Correct observance of KOSHER would require the meat to have been slaughtered by an expert, checked for disease and apportioned in the correct way. Soaking the meat in water or covering it in salt can help reinforce the prohibition on blood and this can be done in the home. There is also a prohibition on consuming milk and meat together, and to this end utensils used for cooking meat are kept distinct from those used for dairy products. (*See also* SHECHITA)

Kavanah   *Lit. attunement.* Intention is an important concept in Judaism and it is necessary that any law be performed with the right intent. A pious Jew should examine his/her motives and the reasons behind the existence of the law to ensure that the law does not become merely a dry performance bereft of meaning. Ideally, it is necessary for the Jew to arrive at a place of attunement to the will of God, from where all the laws will be obeyed in an atmosphere of sanctification. (*See also* MITZVAH)

Kedushah   *Lit. sanctification.* An especially sacred prayer that is offered in the SYNAGOGUE service during the repetition of the AMIDAH that proclaims the holiness, glory and sovereignty of God. The prayer is as follows: 'Holy, Holy, Holy is the Lord of Host; the whole earth is full of His Glory.'

Kehillah   A Jewish community.

Keriah   The tearing of a black ribbon or garment prior to the funeral, allowing the mourner the opportunity to express anguish and anger. This tear is an outward sign of grief and signifies that the mourner is confronting death head-on. The prevailing custom is to tear the ribbon on the mourner's right side, but on the left side (closest to the heart) if grieving for a parent. (*See also* ANINUT; SHIVA; YAHRZEIT)

Ketav Semikhah   A form of ordination into the Rabbinate introduced in fourteenth-century Germany by Meir ha-Levi of Vienna which required all newly qualified rabbis to possess a certificate or writ of ordination (*ketav semikhah*). The practice rapidly spread throughout the Jewish DIASPORA. (*See also* HATTURAT HORAAH; SEMIKHAH)

Keter   The uppermost aspect of the SEFIROTH that can be contemplated by humans. Even so, it is rarely discussed by the followers of KABBALA. Later traditions speak of it radiating 620 'pillars of light' and it is associated with the origin of the will. In mystical states it corresponds to 'nothingness' or the negation of all thought.

Ketubah / Ketubbah   A traditional marriage contract made out by the groom which lists the financial rights of the bride. Today Jews use whatever legal requirements are available in the civil laws of the country of citizenship but there is still a customary reading of the contract by the RABBI after the exchange of the ring. The contract is signed by the witnesses and placed in a safe place. Orthodox rabbis read the entire contract, which may become a crucial document in the event of divorce. (*See also* GET)

Ketuvim   *Lit. holy writings.* The third section of the TANAKH, the Jewish Scripture that consists of the remaining books that are not included in the first five books of MOSES or amongst the books attributed the prophets. These are the twelve books of PSALMS, JOB, Song of Songs, RUTH, LAMENTATIONS, ECCLESIASTES, ESTHER, DANIEL, EZRA, NEHEMIAH and CHRONICLES. (*See also* NEVIIM; TORAH)

Kiddush   A prayer used to sanctify the Sabbath and other holy days. The prayer is recited before the meal on the Friday evening and consists of the recitation of the passages describing the beginning of creation in GENESIS 1.1–3. A short benediction is also given. The prayer is recited over a cup of wine and the Sabbath bread. (*See also* HALLAH; SHABBAT)

Kiddushin   Occurs when a woman accepts the money, contract or sexual relations offered by her prospective husband. The word 'kiddushin' comes from the root *Qof-Dalet-Shin*, meaning 'sanctified', reflecting the sanctity of the marital relation. However, the root word also connotes something that is set aside for a specific (sacred) purpose, and the ritual of kiddushin sets aside a woman to be the wife of a particular man and no other. Kiddushin is far more binding than an engagement, as we understand the term in modern English. Once kiddushin is complete, the woman is legally the wife of the man, and the relationship can only be dissolved by death or divorce. However, the spouses do not live together at the time of the kiddushin, and the mutual obligations created by the marital relationship do not take effect until the NISUIN is complete.

Kippah / Capel   The small skullcap worn by all Orthodox male Jews at all times but by non-Orthodox only during prayers. Two reasons have been given for the wearing of the skullcap. The first is the awareness of the immanence of God in creation through the presence of the SHEKHINA, and therefore the cap is worn out of awe and respect. The second reason concerns the ancient idea that an uncovered head denotes freedom. Jews acknowledge their submission to God through covering their heads. (*See also* YAMULKAH)

Kittel   A traditional white robe worn by some ASHKENAZI Jews on high holy days. It is also part of the clothing in which the dead are buried.

Knesset   *See* BET HA KNESSET.

Kohan / Kohanim   The kohanim are the descendants of AARON, chosen by God at the time of the incident with the Golden Calf to perform certain sacred work, particularly in connection with the animal sacrifices and the rituals related to the TEMPLE. After the destruction of the Temple, the role of the kohanim diminished significantly in favour of the RABBIS. However, Jews continue to keep track of kohein lineage. Kohanim are given the honour of the first opportunity to recite a blessing over the TORAH reading on SHABBAT. They are also required to recite a blessing over the congregation at certain times of the year.

Kohen / Kohenim *See* KOHAN / KOHANIM.

Kol Nidrei / Kol Nidre *Lit. all the vows.* These special prayers are recited on the evening of YOM KIPPUR with deep sincerity and solemnity. God is asked to forgive the petitioners for any promises that were made to Him but not fulfilled. On this special occasion male Jews in the congregation wear the TALLIT (prayer shawl) that is normally worn in the morning prayers.

Korach The name of the leader of the LEVITES who defied MOSES in the wilderness after the release of the Jews from captivity in Egypt. The challenge of the Levites is described in the Book of NUMBERS and arose from the tensions created between the ideal that all the Jews are a sacred people and the new appointment of a special group of priests chosen from the Levites. The laity objected to the priesthood, but Korach tried to demand an even more privileged position for the Levites and was corrected by the appearance of the divine presence. (*See also* SHEKHINA)

Kosher / Kasher Food that is allowed by Jewish dietary laws. (*See also* KASHRUT)

Kvater The Yiddish term for the godmother who is appointed by the parents at the time of circumcision and remains with the child throughout its life as a guide and counsellor. (*See also* KVATERIN; SANDEK)

Kvaterin The Yiddish term for the godfather who is appointed by the parents at the time of circumcision and remains with the child throughout its life as a guide and counsellor. (*See also* KVATER; SANDEK)

L

Ladino A language that was used by Sephardic Jews in the period of the DIASPORA. (*See also* SEPHARDIM)

Lag Ba'Omer A feast day that occurs in the month of Iyyar that is in between the two festivals of PESACH and SHAVUOTH. The festival is a day of celebration, in spite of the fact that the month of Iyyar is associated with sadness and no joyous occasions, such as weddings, are held during this period. The feast day is a popular occasion in ISRAEL, where thousands of people make their way to the city of Safat to visit the tomb of Rabbi Simeon ben Yochai, who defied the decree of the Roman emperor, Hadrian, and continued to teach the TORAH.

Lamentations One of the books of the Holy Scriptures that belongs to the section known as the Holy Writings. Traditionally, the elegiac text is attributed to the prophet JEREMIAH, writing after the destruction of the TEMPLE in JERUSALEM. The complete book is usually read in the SYNAGOGUE on the fast that takes place on the ninth day of the month of Av. The day of fast is held primarily to mourn the loss of the Temple. (*See also* KETUVIM)

Lashon ha-kodesh *Lit. holy tongue. See* IVRIT.

Leah The sister of RACHEL who was given to JACOB in marriage by her cunning father, Laban, who veiled her so that Jacob was tricked into believing that he was marrying Rachel, the woman he loved and to win whose hand he had served her father for seven years. It is still the custom in Jewish weddings that the groom lifts the veil of his bride in private just before the public ceremony in order that the same error is not made. (*See also* KETUBAH)

Lekhah Dodi   The hymn composed by Solomon Alkabetz of Safat, a RABBI of the KABBALA tradition, to celebrate the arrival of the Sabbath. In the city of Safat in Galilee, the great centre of Jewish mystical practice, it was the tradition to welcome the Sabbath as a bride by dressing in white on the Sabbath eve and going out into the fields rejoicing. The hymn begins 'Come, my beloved, to meet the Bride' and is now sung in all SYNAGOGUES on the Sabbath eve. (*See also* EREV SHABBAT; SHABBAT)

Levirate marriage   The scriptural requirement that a man should marry the widow of his brother if their marriage was childless.

Levites   The priests appointed to attend the sanctuary after its establishment by MOSES. They were appointed from the tribe of Levi and developed as a wandering priesthood with little institutionalization. The basic pattern was that a Levite chose to become a priest and then wandered free of tribal affiliation searching for a local sanctuary where he could be employed. Later they became priests at the TEMPLE in JERUSALEM.

Leviticus   The third of the five books of the Jewish Scriptures that comprise the TORAH or PENTATEUCH. It focuses on laws of ritual and purity. Leviticus means LEVITES, and the book details their sacred duties in the sanctuary along with rules concerning diet, purification, festivals and marriage.

Lilith   The belief that God gave Adam a first wife before Eve, named Lilith, who was created his equal, as in the Genesis verse: 'And God created man in his own image, in the image of God He created him; male and female He created them' (GENESIS 1.27). She was pursued by Adam's son and returned to dust. The mystical tradition states that Lilith stood before God and demanded absolute equality, pronouncing the sacred name of God that is forbidden. As a result she was made a demon to haunt mankind. It is said that Lilith tries to tempt men through the power of women and inspired the serpent to tempt Eve in the Garden of Eden.

Lot   The brother of ABRAHAM, as recounted in the Book of GENESIS, who led his people into the wicked cities of Sodom and Gomorrah and was reluctant to leave when warned that God intended to destroy them. His wife looked back longingly on the cities and was turned into a pillar of salt.

Lubavitch   An ultra-Orthodox group based in the USA and, until his death, led by Lubavitcher Rebbe, a great Hasidic leader, who some followers regarded as the Messiah. The Lubavitcher are active in missionary work amongst lapsed Jews and have developed a chain of Jewish schools that combine secular and Orthodox education. They have also established student centres in American universities to promote Orthodox practice. (*See also* HASIDIM)

Lulav   The practice of waving palm leaves in all directions during the recital of HALLEL that takes place on the festival of SUKKOT. The practice dates back to the time of the TEMPLE in JERUSALEM, where the priests made a circumambulation of the altar waving palm leaves. (*See also* ARBA MINIM)

M

Maariv   The final of the three obligatory daily prayers that is offered after nightfall. The prayer is believed to have been instituted by JACOB. Sometimes in the SYNAGOGUE, the afternoon and evening prayers are combined to save visiting twice in a short period of time. The *Maariv* service consists of a few verses from the PSALMS, some blessings, the SHEMA, several more blessings, the silent AMIDAH and then the ALEINU to conclude. (*See also* MINHAH; SHAHARIT)

Maccabees   The Jewish family which led the rebellion against Antiochus V Ephiphanes and the Seleucids in 165 BCE under the leadership of Judas Maccabees. The Maccabees succeeded in capturing JERUSALEM and in restoring the TEMPLE. This event is celebrated at the Festival of HANUKKAH.

Machzor   *Lit. cycle of prayers.* The prayer book used only for festivals which contains prayers and the readings from the TORAH and the books of the Prophets that are prescribed for the days of the festivals. (*See also* PESACH; SHAVUOTH; SUKKOT; SYNAGOGUE)

Magen David   The six-pointed Star or Shield of DAVID that is used in the flag of ISRAEL and often presented as the symbol of Judaism.

Mahzor   An ASHKENAZI term for the prayer books that provide the annual cycle of prayers recited at festivals.

Maimonides   Rabbi Moses ben Maimon (1135–1204 CE). Famous philosopher, physician and codifier of Jewish law, respected by both Christians and Muslims. After leaving Spain, he lived in Cairo as the court physician to the Muslim sultan of the Fatimid dynasty. Maimonides introduced Aristotelian philosophical thought to Jewish philosophy and provided Jewish rationalism with a classical foundation. He combined a systematic approach to the organization of human knowledge based on reason with the religious tradition based on revelation and the Bible. His main philosophical work was the *Guide to the Perplexed* and his brief thirteen principles of the Jewish faith have come to be regarded as creed and appear in simplified form in the liturgy of the SYNAGOGUE. Maimonides' principles of faith are as follows:

> *God is the Creator of the Universe*
> *God is One*
> *God has no body, form or likeness*
> *God is eternal. There was never a time when He did not exist, and there will never be a time when He will cease to exist*
> *One must pray only to God*
> *God revealed himself to the Prophets*
> *The Torah was given by God to Moses*
> *The Torah is eternal; God will not change the Torah, nor will he allow the Torah to be superseded*
> *God knows all the thoughts and all the deeds of the people*
> *God rewards those who keep His laws and punishes those who disobey them*
> *God will send His Messiah to usher in a new and better world*
> *God will revive the dead.*

Makum Kadosh   *Lit. holy place.* The term is generally used for the TEMPLE and the SYNAGOGUE.

Malachi   A prophet with a book named after him included in the Jewish Scriptures. He preached against the innovations and corruptions that were creeping into temple worship after the Second TEMPLE was completed in 516 BCE. Malachi blamed the priests and the LEVITES and appeals to ISRAEL to obey the TORAH. (*See also* NEVIIM)

Malkhut   According to the tradition of the KABBALA, the last of the ten SEFIROTH that emanate from the AYN SOF. The source of God's sovereignty, it manifests itself in the material creation or realms of existence that exist below the levels of the *sefiroth*.

Mamzer   The child of an adulterous or incestuous sexual encounter.

Mappah   *Lit. tablecloth.* Notes added to the SHULHAN ARUKH by Rabbi Moses Isserles of Cracow that made Joseph Caro's influential compilation of the law acceptable to ASHKENAZI Jews.

Maror   One of the bitter herbs eaten in the SEDER or Passover meal.

Mashiach   *See* MESSIACH.

Maskilim   A group of eighteenth-century Jews who upheld the principles of the Enlightenment and insisted that Jews should come out of the ghetto mentally, spiritually and physically and combine their religious practice and belief with science, education and the arts. They were influenced by Moses Mendelssohn and the HASKALAH.

Masorah   The present text of the Jewish Scriptures that has been carefully preserved by the scribes. The text was the work of the Masorites, Palestinian scholars of the biblical text around the sixth to eighth centuries BCE. They explored the text, noting every Hebrew letter, the frequency of unusual words, parallels in the text and searched for variant readings which were noted in the margins. (*See also* TANAKH; TORAH)

Masorites   *See* MASORAH.

Massiach / Mashiach / Moshiach / Messiah   The anointed one awaited by the Jews, who will come to bring deliverance and usher in a new era for the world. Since the destruction of the TEMPLE, Jews have been comforted by the belief that one day God would forgive them and allow them to return to the Holy Land of ISRAEL. In this time of redemption, the whole world would be transformed into the Kingdom of God and war and human conflict would disappear. The original Messianic ideal seems to have been expressed in the belief that the kingdom of Israel would be reunited as it was at the time of DAVID. The Jews began to hope for a king in the line of David who would restore the kingdom to its original glory. At the same time, prophets such as ISAIAH were beginning to speak about a future age when God's kingdom would reign on the earth. These two ideas dovetailed after the DIASPORA in 70 CE. Orthodox Jews certainly regard the Messiah as more than a political figure; the usual understanding is of a human being with special spiritual powers from God. However, the Temple in JERUSALEM will be restored and the Davidic kingdom of Israel will be re-established. Human beings will live in peace and harmony with each other under obedience to God's commandments as expressed in the TORAH. This period of peace and prosperity will then be followed by the Day of Judgement.

Matzah / Matzot   The unleavened bread used during the Passover when the consumption of yeast is prohibited. This refers back to the bread that was eaten by the Israelites in their flight from Egypt after being released from slavery. They were in such a hurry to depart that there was no time to bake leavened bread. (*See also* PESACH; SEDER)

Megillah   A term used for a scroll of sacred texts, particularly the Book of ESTHER, read at the festival of PURIM.

Megilloth   Five of the books that belong to the section of the Jewish Scriptures known as Holy Writings which are read on special occasions in the SYNAGOGUE. They are the Song of Songs, RUTH, LAMENTATIONS, ECCLESIASTES and ESTHER. (*See also* KETUVIM)

Mehitsah   A barrier that separates men from women in traditional or Orthodox SYNAGOGUES.

Mekhilta   The MIDRASH that deals with the Book of EXODUS.

Menorah   The eight-branched candelabrum used at the feast of HANUKKAH and that was previously lit daily in the TEMPLE in JERUSALEM.

Mezuzah A small scroll placed on the doorposts of Jewish homes and the entrance to the living room on which is written the first two paragraphs of the SHEMA. It is contained in a small narrow case with an opening in the back which is placed on the right-hand doorpost about two-thirds of the way up. It is positioned diagonally so that the upper end inclines towards the house or room. The Mezuzah is commanded in the Book of DEUTERONOMY which states: 'And you shall write them upon the doorposts of your house and upon your gates.' The Mezuzah functions to remind Jews that they are under God's protection and guidance, but it is also simply an indicator of identity.

Micah A prophet and a book of the Jewish Scriptures that is named after him. A younger contemporary of ISAIAH, he condemned the corruption and tyranny of the judges, aristocracy and false prophets in the kingdom of Judah. Micah provides prophecies that tell of the coming of the Messiah. (*See also* MASSIACH; NEVIIM)

Midrash The practice of interpretation of Scripture that developed into collections of rabbinic commentaries on the Hebrew Bible. They deal with legal matters but also expound on scriptural narrative. The difference between Midrash and MISHNAH is that the latter need not refer to Scripture, as it is based on oral tradition. The early Tannaitic Midrash, written in the first two centuries CE, consist of interpretations of the books of EXODUS, LEVITICUS, NUMBERS and DEUTERONOMY. In the later Amoraic period, far freer and more far-fetched interpretations of Scripture were produced that contained a compilation of hagiographic accounts of rabbinical behaviour. The best known of these collections, together with the earlier work on the TORAH, are known as Midrash Rabbah or 'the Great Midrash'.

Mikvah A special pool that must be filled with water that has been in contact with either a stream or rainwater. Tap water may be added once an amount of 'living water' has been collected. Traditionally the pool must contain a minimum of 240 gallons of water. At one time, all traditional Jewish communities would have contained a bathhouse for the performance of *mikvah*, the ritual bathing. It is still used in ORTHODOX JUDAISM for the ritual cleansing of women after menstruation; the submersion of converts as a rite of passage into Judaism; by women on the eve of their marriage; and by Jews who had been in contact with anything that was considered defiling, such as a dead body. (*See also* NIDDAH)

Milah   *See* BERIT MILAH.

Minhah   The middle of the three obligatory prayers that is recited in the afternoon. Traditionally believed to have been instituted by ISAAC, it is named after the meal offering made in the TEMPLE in JERUSALEM. The prayer is offered during the second half of the day and must take place between nine and a half and eleven and a half hours after daybreak. The service opens with Psalm 145, the half-KADDISH followed by a silent AMIDAH and confession, and ends with ALEINU. (*See also* MAARIV; SHAHARIT)

Minyan   Congregational prayer is very important in Judaism, and it is said that whenever Jews are gathered together in prayer, the SHEKHINA, the divine presence, is there amongst them. It is also written in the TALMUD that a man's prayers are heard by God only when he prays as part of a congregation. The RABBIS have agreed that a group of at least ten men is required to hold a Jewish service whenever the most sacred prayers of Judaism are recited, such as the AMIDAH or the KADDISH, and the TORAH scrolls are read. Some progressive communities now include women in the *Minyan*. (*See also* SEFER TORAH; SYNAGOGUE; TEFILLAH)

Misheberakh   A SYNAGOGUE blessing bestowed on those who are called to read from the TORAH. It also includes their family members.

Mishkan   The original travelling sanctuary used by the Jewish nomadic tribes before the building of the TEMPLE in JERUSALEM. The Book of EXODUS relates how the Jews would set up the sanctuary in their encampments in the desert, placing it in the centre of an open courtyard, surrounded by a fence covered with cloth. Inside this courtyard was the Holy of Holies that contained the ARK OF THE COVENANT.

Mishnah   The original writing down of the oral TORAH tradition, that now forms part of the TALMUD. It is divided into various sections: Zeraim, deals with agricultural laws; Moed, which deals with festivals and the Sabbath; Nashim, which deals with matters concerning women, particularly the laws of marriage; Nezikin, which deals with legal matters such as commerce and criminal law; Kadashim, which deals with the sacrificial system and Taharot, which deals with matters of ritual impurities. The writing down of the oral tradition that represented the teachings of Jewish sages throughout history was achieved from the first century BCE through to Judah ha-Nasi's compilation in the second century CE. It is believed that the oral law was revealed to MOSES and passed down through a direct line of transmission to the PHARISEES, who oversaw the beginning of the writing down of the Mishnah. In the fourth century CE, the teachings of these RABBIS were collected and incorporated into the Palestinian Talmud. In the sixth century CE, the great rabbinical colleges in Babylon created the Babylonian Talmud. Both Talmuds essentially contain the Mishnah. Explanations are provided of laws, inconsistencies between interpretations are resolved and any laws that have become redundant are explained.

Mishpatim   The laws in the TORAH that are considered accessible to reason or whose *raison d'etre* is not transparent. (*See also* MITZVAH)

Mitzvah / Mitzvot   *Lit. commandment.* Just as TORAH refers to Jewish observance as a totality, a mitzvah refers to an individual instruction or obligation required by God of the Jews. The compilers of the TALMUD divided mitzvah into two categories: *mitzvot aseh* – the commands to perform an action; and *mitzvot lo ta'aseh* – the commands to refrain from a certain action. The aim of both kinds of commandment is to promote sanctity, and traditional Jews will recite a blessing before performing a mitzvah: 'blessed art Thou, O Lord, King of the Universe, who has sanctified us with His commandments and has commanded us to...' Another division of mitzvah made by rabbinical commentators is *hukkim* – those commandments that are clear or easily understood; and MISHPATIM – those whose meaning is unclear and have to be accepted without understanding the rationale behind them although clarity can be sought through the use of reason. Of the 613 laws revealed by God to MOSES, 248 were positive and 365 were negative, but laws have also been added to the original law of Moses throughout Jewish history as specific historical events have arisen. There are also laws pertaining to worship in the TEMPLE in JERUSALEM that can no longer be followed since its destruction in 70 CE.

Mohel   A religious person trained to perform the ritual of circumcision. Today modern surgical instruments are used. At the circumcision, the *mohel* stands before two chairs. In one chair, the child is held by his godfather; the other is the chair of ELIJAH, the prophet who is the guardian of ISRAEL. The child is given to the *mohel*, who places him in Elijah's chair and makes a benediction. He is then handed back to the godfather and the ritual circumcision takes place on the godfather's lap. The *mohel* recites all the blessings throughout the ritual. (*See also* BERIT MILAH; SANDEK)

Moses   The leader and law-giver of ISRAEL at the time of the EXODUS from Israel. Born a Jew in captivity, his parents had floated him down the River Nile where the daughter of Pharaoh discovered him in the bulrushes. He was brought up as a prince of Egypt but had to flee after killing an Egyptian who was ill-treating a Jewish slave. God appointed him a prophet after appearing in the Burning Bush and commanded him to free the Jews from captivity. Moses received the revelation of the law on Mount Sinai after leading the people out of Egypt. Most traditional Jews believe that Moses received both the written and the oral TORAH from God and passed them both down through an unbroken chain of transmission through JOSHUA, the elders, the prophets and finally to the RABBIS. The first five books of the Scriptures are known as the Books of Moses. The seventh day of the month of Adar is observed in commemoration of Moses' death.

Moshiach   *See* MASSIACH.

Musar   *Lit. instruction or reproof.* These are ethical works that call Jews to live a better life based on God's commandments in the

TORAH, the voice of conscience and social duty. During the Middle Ages many *Musar* were produced such as Rabbi Bahya's *Duties of the Heart*. However, the *Musar* movement was founded in the nineteenth century in Lithuania by Rabbi Israel Lipkin. He introduced the idea of consistent chanting of the *Musar* literature so that it sank down into the depths of the being, without which it had little impact and the transformation of character did not take place. The *Musarists* have had considerable impact in the education of Jews in the YESHIVA of the USA and ISRAEL.

Mussaf An additional prayer to the obligatory three daily prayers that is recited on the Sabbath and festival days and believed to date back to traditional practices at the TEMPLE in JERUSALEM. (*See also* MAARIV; MINHAH; SHAHARIT)

N

Nahmanides   A thirteenth-century RABBI otherwise known as Moses Ben Nahman, a kabbalist, who provided substantial exegesis of the sacred texts. He posited the idea of an eternal TORAH that was only recorded by Moses. He also disputed MAIMONIDES' emphasis on the afterlife being the immortality of the soul and preferred to emphasize the resurrection of the body. (*See also* KABBALA; OLAM-HA-BA)

Nahum   One of the twelve 'minor' prophets and a book of the same name in the Jewish Scritures. Nahum's prophecies mainly dwell on the fate that would befall the Assyrian empire because of their cruelty. He preached that there was a divine code of righteous behaviour that all humanity had to observe and that all those nations that failed to observe it would eventually be doomed. The main brunt of his prophecy is levelled against the Assyrian capital, Ninevah, which eventually fell in 612 BCE. (*See also* NEVIIM)

Naomi   The mother-in-law of RUTH who is regarded as the ideal of the righteous convert. In ORTHODOX JUDAISM, a set of questions and answers attributed to Ruth and Naomi are used in the process of conversion. (*See also* GER)

Nathan   The Jewish prophet who lived at the same time as DAVID. He criticized David on several occasions when the king departed from the moral code expected of a lover of God. In particular, he criticized the king for introducing the innovation of a permanent TEMPLE in

JERUSALEM when formerly the God of the Israelites had been worshipped by a travelling people in the desert.

Nathan, Rabbi   A prominent RABBI and scholar from the period of the fourth generation of TANNAIM (139–165 CE) in Babylon after the exile from ISRAEL by the Romans. He was a significant contributor to the development of the MISHNAH but remained in opposition to the authorities in Rome, unlike many of the fifth generation of Tannaim. (*See also* ABOT DI RABBI NATHAN)

Nehemiah   One of the books of the Hebrew Scriptures known as Holy Writings. Nehemiah was the cup-bearer of Artoxerxes, the King of Babylon. He managed to secure permission to return to JERUSALEM and in 444 BCE was appointed Military Governor of Judea. He worked with EZRA to ensure that the Jewish people obeyed the TORAH and oversaw the rebuilding of the walls of the city. (*See also* KETUVIM; TANAKH)

Neilah   *Lit. closing.* The last of the five services held in the SYNAGOGUE on YOM KIPPUR. The title may refer to the closing of the gates of the TEMPLE in JERUSALEM after the evening prayers, whilst others maintain that it refers to closing the gates of heaven. The congregation petition God to answer their prayers and seal them in the Book of Life. The service ends with reciting the last verse of the SHEMA.

Ner Tamid   *Lit. eternal light.* The lamp which is kept burning above the ARK in the SYNAGOGUE and represents the light that was kept in the sanctuary of the TEMPLE in JERUSALEM.

Netzah   *Lit. victory.* According to the tradition of the KABBALA, the eighth of the ten SEFIROTH who emanate from the AYN SOF. It is the third on the right-hand side of the Tree of Life and, along with HOD, is one of the two supports for the *sefiroth*.

Neviim   The books ascribed to the Prophets in the Hebrew Scriptures that appear in the second section. They are divided into two parts: the early prophets and the later prophets. The first part deals with the prophets SAMUEL, NATHAN, Ahijah, ELIJAH and Elisha, and consists of the books of JOSHUA, JUDGES, the two books of Samuel and the two books of Kings. The second part is also divided into major and minor prophets – the division is not qualitative but simply refers to the size of the books. The major prophets are ISAIAH, EZEKIAL and JEREMIAH. The twelve minor prophets are HOSEA, JOEL, AMOS, OBADIAH, JONAH, MICAH, NAHUM, HABUKKUK, ZEPHANIAH, HAGGAI, ZECHARIAH and MALACHI. In the Hebrew Scriptures the last twelve are considered as one book because of the brevity of the material. In Judaism, the prophets are the carriers of revelation; they are human beings called upon by God to be His messengers. They preached in God's name, moved by His spirit, and called upon the people to obey God's law. They also warned of the consequences of disobedience. (*See also* TANAKH; TORAH)

Niddah   *Lit. she who is separated.* The laws contained in the TORAH regarding the separation of women during menstruation and after giving birth. In ORTHODOX JUDAISM, a woman in this condition may not sleep with her husband or attend the SYNAGOGUE. The rabbis interpreted the law to state that a woman remains unclean for seven days after the flow of blood has stopped. After childbirth, she is impure for 14 days after the birth of a boy and 21 days after the birth of a girl. After the period of impurity, she attends the ritual bath. (*See also* MIKVAH)

Niddui   Excommunication from the community, used as a prominent form of punishment by Jewish courts in the territories of Islam, where sentences of execution or capital punishment were only permitted by the governing bodies. They were also used as a punishment for individuals who disobeyed TAKKANOT, or decrees issued by the community.

Nisuin   The completion of the process of marriage, derived from a word meaning 'elevation'. The husband brings his wife into his home and they begin their married life together. (*See also* KIDDUSHIN)

Noachide Laws   The seven laws that form the foundation of a just human society. They were revealed by God to NOAH at the end of the flood and form part of the covenant made between God and Noah. The seven laws are usually depicted as:

1. To worship only the one God and to renounce all idol worship.
2. To live a moral life and not commit adultery or incest.
3. To live as a useful member of society and not commit murder.
4. To be honest and not steal.
5. To have respect for God and not blaspheme.
6. To provide courts of law and a system of justice to maintain society.
7. To be kind to animals and to refrain from cruelty.

Noah   The patriarch chosen by God to save a remnant of the people and a sample of all the earth's creatures during the great flood. This is achieved by the building of a great ark. Noah is regarded as the father of all people born after the flood and the revelation made to him is for all humanity rather than only the Jewish people. One of the three covenants is made with Noah but, unlike the other two, it is not exclusive to the Jews. (*See also* BERIT; NOACHIDE LAWS)

Numbers   The fourth of the five books of the TORAH or PENTATEUCH which tells of the wanderings in the wilderness after liberation from slavery in Egypt. The title refers to the numbering of the people that was carried out in the wilderness.

Obadiah One of the twelve minor prophets and a book of the same name in the Jewish Scriptures. The book consists of only one chapter, which rails against the people of Edom for handing over fugitive Jews to the Babylonians after the invasion of Nebuchadnezzar in 586 BCE. (*See also* NEVIIM)

Olam ha-ba The belief in the afterlife. Judaism refers to the world beyond this life in two ways: the immortality of the soul and the resurrection of the body. Traditionally, the Jewish belief in the afterlife is connected with the coming of the Messiah. After His kingdom on earth, the dead will be resurrected. However, NAHMANIDES believed that the resurrected bodies would live forever, albeit refined. MAIMONIDES argued that only the soul was immortal, so eventually even the resurrected bodies would die. The mystical tradition affirms a blissful eternity spent in proximity to God. There is very little in the Bible to affirm an afterlife and Judaism has been called a 'this-worldly' religion that focuses on a godly and just life here on earth. (*See also* GEHENNA)

Oleh A Jew who migrates to ISRAEL.

Omer A seven-week solemn period between the festivals of PESACH and SUKKOT.

Oneg Shabbat *Lit. the delight of the Sabbath.* The positive aspects of the weekly SHABBAT, in which Jews attempt to rediscover the peace and tranquility of God by having a day that combines festivity and spirituality. The expression comes from Isaiah 58.13 'And call the Sabbath a delight'.

Onen   A mourner in the period that precedes a Jewish funeral.

Orthodox Judaism   The term used for traditional Jews who observe both the written and oral law in its entirety, particularly ritual laws. They implicitly believe that the TORAH is the revealed word of God and cannot be tampered with by human interference. The term 'Orthodox' was originally coined by the REFORM movement as a term of reproach but was adopted by those that were criticized as backward-looking as a form of pride in their conservative stance.

P

Parashah   In Sephardic Judaism, the weekly cycle of readings from the TORAH maintained in the SYNAGOGUE. (*See also* SEPHARDIM)

Parev / Pareve / Parvah   A part of the KASHRUT or Jewish dietary laws. It refers to neutral foods that are neither milk nor meat. Fruit would be an example. (*See also* KOSHER)

Parokhet   The curtain hung in front of the ARK in a SYNAGOGUE that represents the veil hung over the original ARK OF THE COVENANT as described in EXODUS 26.31–33.

Parshat / Parshiot   The passages of the TORAH that are apportioned for each reading in the SYNAGOGUE throughout the Jewish year. At each section, a member of the congregation will be called, recite a blessing and provide the reading in Hebrew from the Torah scrolls, then offer a final blessing at the end of the section. (*See also* ALIYAH)

Parvah   *See* PAREV.

Passover   *See* PESACH.

Pentateuch   The first five books of the Hebrew Scriptures: GENESIS, EXODUS, DEUTERONOMY, LEVITICUS and NUMBERS, known as the Books of MOSES. (*See also* SEPTUAGINT; TORAH)

Pesach / Pessah   The spring festival held in the month of Adar, after PURIM, that celebrates the EXODUS from Egypt and is regarded as the national birthday of the foundation of the Jewish people. The festival is known as Passover, to commemorate the scriptural account of the destruction of the firstborn of Egypt that did not affect the children of ISRAEL, as promised by God. The angels literally passed over them. The significant feature of the festival is the SEDER meal, which is ritually eaten according to the instructions contained in the HAGADAH. The festival is observed for eight days (seven in Israel) and each day has its own sequence of events. On the first day, the TORAH reading is from the Book of Exodus and tells the story of the origins of the festival, the death of the firstborn and the flight from Egypt; the second day is the same as the first, but the reading concerns the foundation of the Jewish festivals as instituted in the Torah. From the third day, the songs of praise in the SYNAGOGUE are shortened in order to remember the suffering of the Egyptians, as the Jews are commanded to be a compassionate people. On the Sabbath, known as HOL HA-MOED, the Torah reading introduces God's 13 attributes of mercy and the Song of Songs is read, with the emphasis on spring and renewal. On the seventh day the Torah reading recounts the drowning of the Egyptians in the Red Sea. (*See also* SEUDATH; MITZVAH)

Pharisees   The founders of modern rabbinical Judaism, this important Jewish movement was formed in the second century BCE and was known for its strict observance of the TORAH. They differ from the SADDUCEES, their great rivals, in the great emphasis they place on the oral tradition as well as the written Torah. This unwritten corpus of traditional lore was known as the 'tradition of the fathers' and became part of Jewish discourse and interpretation, used to formulate law. The other major difference between the Pharisees and the Sadducees is the acknowledgement by the former of an afterlife, whether it be heaven or hell.

Pidyon Ha-Ben   A ritual ceremony performed when the first child is a son and not born into a Kohen or Levi lineage. The rite goes back to the belief that God had originally intended all the firstborn males to be His priests but this was overturned because they joined in with the worship of the Golden Calf after release from Egypt. Consequently their birthright was given to the tribe of Levi, who refrained from idol worship. Therefore the firstborn males have to be released from this obligation in a ceremony that takes place 30 days after birth. The child is brought on a pillow by his mother up to a table laid with HALLAH and a KIDDUSH cup. His father stands at the table with five silver coins ready to give to a Kohen, a member of the priestly caste, who stands facing him. The child is ransomed to free him of his obligation to become a priest. The ceremony ends with a MITZVAH meal. Some non-Orthodox Jews perform the ceremony for all children as a mark of gratitude for the gift of a first child. (*See also* LEVITES)

Pikei Avot / Pirke Avoth   *Lit. sayings of the fathers.* Part of the MISHNAH, which contains the ethical teachings of rabbinical sages.

Pikuakh Nefesh   The permitted setting aside of certain laws (HALAKHAH) if by doing so it is possible to save a life.

Pirke Avoth   *See* PIKEI AVOT.

Piyyutim   Liturgical poetry written by medieval poets for special occasions, such as Jewish festivals, which may be added to prayers so long as the established framework of ritual prayer is not changed. (*See also* TEFILLAH)

Pogrom   Organized persecutions of Jews, particularly those that took place in Eastern Europe and Russia from the Middle Ages through to the nineteenth century. The systematic and periodic persecution of Jewish communities culminated in the Holocaust. (*See also* SHOAH)

Proverbs   A book of the Jewish Scriptures that appears in the section known as Holy Writings. They stress the importance of wisdom and provide maxims for right conduct in daily life. They are attributed to SOLOMON and are regarded as proof of his reputed wisdom. (*See also* KETUVIM)

Psalms   Of the 150 Psalms, a book of the Jewish Scriptures, Jews believe that 73 were written by DAVID. The Psalms were sung in the TEMPLE in JERUSALEM by the LEVITES until its destruction by the Romans. For example, 15 Psalms were sung on the festival of SUKKOT and one Psalm introduced the daily morning sacrifice. Today Psalms are used in daily prayer and on some occasions in the SYNAGOGUE.

Purim   A spring festival held in the month of Adar (1 February – 18 March) that remembers the success of ESTHER in preventing the massacre of Persian Jews as recounted in the Book of Esther. On the eve of the festival, traditional Jews will attend the SYNAGOGUE, still fasting from the one-day fast known as the 'Fast of Esther'. Two plates are kept at the entrance to the synagogue; one for a silver coin and the other for an offering to the poor. The TORAH reading will include the Book of Esther. The children attending the synagogue will shake rattles every time the name of Haman, the wicked vizier, is mentioned. At dinner and throughout the day, special pastries known as *Hamentaschen* or 'Haman's hat' are eaten. At the morning synagogue service, verses from the MEGILLAH are recited and afterwards gifts of food are exchanged by the congregation. A special banquet takes place in the afternoon where much drinking of alcohol is permitted. In ISRAEL, children will go from house to house in fancy dress.

R

Rabbi   *Lit. my master.* The title given to an authorized Jewish teacher who has been trained and examined in Jewish religious law. Rabbis are the religious leaders of the Jewish people and historically they have provided the textual interpretations and commentaries on the Jewish Scriptures that provide the manuals for correct Jewish practice. (*See also* SYNAGOGUE)

Rachel   The wife of the patriarch JACOB, who served her father for seven years in order to win her hand. After Rachel's father tricked him into marrying her sister LEAH, Jacob served for another seven years, finally winning the hand of Rachel.

Rashi, Rabbi   Otherwise known as Rabbi Schlomo ben Yitzhak (1045–1105) a leading commentator on the TORAH and TALMUD whose work is considered indispensable in understanding the Torah. He provides commentary not only on passages, but also on individual phrases and separate words.

Rebbe   *Rabbi.* The respectful but affectionate title used by Hasidic Jews for their religious leaders or *zadeks*. (*See also* HASIDIM; ZADDIKIM)

Reform Judaism   The Reform movement originated in nineteenth-century Germany from the questioning of traditional Judaism which arose as a response to the challenge of Western society and developments in science, education and technology. German Jews were concerned with the number leaving the practice of their faith as a result of the influence of contemporary cultural thinking. The reformers felt that while Judaism had much to offer, it had to come to terms with the modern world. Originally the pace of reform was slow and resulted only in minor changes, such as prayers in the vernacular language. The basic tenet of the Reform Jews is that the ethical laws of Judaism are eternal and immutable but the ritual laws can be adapted to modern life and even replaced altogether. Consequently, the traditions of divorce, dietary laws, the role of women, dress, SYNAGOGUE practices and even the maintenance of the Sabbath have all come under scrutiny. The Reform tradition came to prominence in the USA and Western Europe. (*See also* ORTHODOX JUDAISM)

Responsa   *See* SHEELOT U-TESHUVOT.

Rishonim   *Lit. the early ones.* The writers of the earlier codes of law that preceded the setting down of the authoritative SHULHAN ARUKH written by Rabbi Caro (1488–1575). They are considered to have more authority than the later commentators who can only overrule a decision made by one of them if it is possible to find another *Rishon* to support the new interpretation or addition. (*See also* AHARONIM)

Rosh Hashanah / Rosh Ha-Shanah   The festival of the Jewish New Year which remembers God's act of creating the world. It is followed by the Ten Days of Penitence which culminate in the Day of Atonement (YOM KIPPUR) and thus it marks the beginning of the most sacred part of the Jewish religious calendar. It is believed that all human beings will pass before God on the New Year and it is at this time that the Book of Judgement is updated and sealed on Yom Kippur, ten days later. In the SYNAGOGUE, the PAROKHET, the reading desk and the TORAH scroll mantles are all decked in white and the RABBI, cantor, and the blower of the SHOFAR are all dressed in white robes. The shofar is blown 30 times at three places within the ceremony and the service consists of the MUSSAF, *Malkhuyyot* and ZIKHRONOT and specific readings from the three sections of the

Bible, the Torah, the NEVIIM and the KETUVIM. The Torah readings are primarily concerned with the binding of ISAAC. In the home a piece of bread is dipped in honey and eaten. This is followed by an apple and a prayer that the year ahead will be sweet.

Rosh Hodesh   *Lit. the head of the month.* A minor festival that occurs at the beginning of each Jewish month. There is no work prohibition and the festival is celebrated in the SYNAGOGUE by a reading of the HALLEL and the TORAH. Four people are called up for the reading and then the festive prayer or MUSSAF is recited to bless the following month. Traditionally, the holiday is regarded as honouring women for their superior piety.

Ruah ha-kodesh   The holy spirit of God that is bestowed upon the righteous or pious person who has attained various stages of progress in his/her spiritual life through his/her own efforts and love for God. The holy spirit is the gift of holiness or saintliness.

Ruth   A book of the Jewish Scriptures that belongs in the section known as Holy Writings. It tells the story of Ruth of the Moabites who loved a Jew named Boaz, whom she met in the fields during the harvest season. Ruth is regarded as the perfect convert. The answers that she gave to the questions posed by her mother-in-law, NAOMI, remain the test for the Jewish convert in Orthodoxy. The Book of Ruth is read during the festival of SHAVUOT. (*See also* GER)

S

Sadducees   Conservative priests and their followers who became prominent in the first centuries BCE and CE in ISRAEL. They believed only in the written law and denied the oral law, and were opposed to the idea of any kind of afterlife. (*See also* OLAM HA-BA; PHARISEES; TORAH)

Samaritans   The inhabitants of Samaria who are regarded with intense suspicion and dislike by the Jews. The Samaritans built their own temple on Mount Gerizim. There remains a small community in modern ISRAEL which is monotheistic and accepts only the prophethood of Moses.

Samson   The thirteenth Judge of ISRAEL, who held the position for 20 years. Born to a childless couple, his birth was announced by an angel and the spirit of God was with him. Samson was renowned for his great strength and his exploits against the Philistines. He was eventually betrayed to the Philistines by Delilah, who cut his hair which resulted in the loss of his strength. (*See also* JUDGES)

Samuel   Two books of the Jewish Scriptures that appear in the first part of the section known as the Prophets, where the early prophets are recorded. The books of Samuel recount the life of the prophet of the same name and the rise of the monarchy from the appointment of SAUL as ISRAEL's first king through to the reign of his successor, DAVID. (*See also* NEVIIM)

Sandek   The godfather allocated by the parents to a male child and who accompanies him to his circumcision when eight days old. The godfather has the honour of holding the child after the benedictions and during the actual operation. The godparents are also appointed to function as counsellors to the child throughout their lives. (*See also* BERIT MILAH)

Sanhedrin   The highest Jewish court that met in JERUSALEM. It ceased to function sometime around 425 CE. Its RABBIS were instrumental in developing and interpreting the MISHNAH, and until its disbanding they were responsible for determining the Jewish lunar calendar. As soon as the new moon rose, they dispatched messengers throughout the land of ISRAEL to announce the date. They also made the decision to celebrate the festivals over two days to accommodate the DIASPORA communities who could not be informed by the messengers. The practice of a two-day celebration is still observed (*See also* YOMTOV SHENI)

Satan   *Lit. the accuser.* Although he plays that role in the Book of Job, generally Judaism does not give a prominent role to the idea of a personification of evil, even though the belief in demons and a hell realm has existed in Jewish folk tradition. The separate existence of an all-powerful demonic force would undermine the central tenet of Jewish monotheism.

Saul   The first king of ISRAEL around the year 1050 BCE. It is usually suggested that the pressure to become a monarchy arose from the warlike excursions of the Philistines who could not be defeated by tribal alliances. It was the loss of the ARK OF THE COVENANT to the Philistines at the Battle of Aphek, where the forces of Israel were defeated, that led to calls for a king. Saul had proven his military and charismatic qualities in fighting the Ammonites, and the people asked the prophet SAMUEL to anoint Saul as a king. (*See also* DAVID; SOLOMON)

Savoraim   *Lit. expounders.* The term used for the rabbinical commentators who contributed to the Babylonian TALMUD after the Muslims conquered Babylon in the tenth century CE. There were two famous schools at Sura and Pumpedita. The leaders were known as GEONIM and the first qualification was to know the Talmud by heart. They are partly responsible for the Babylonian Talmud becoming the authoritative version in Jewish life. (*See also* AMORAIM)

Seder The home-based ritual meal maintained at the Passover festival which has been celebrated since the night before the EXODUS from Egypt. It is one of the most important events in the Jewish religious calendar. The story of the escape from Egypt, as described in the book of Exodus, is told to Jewish children, who ask a number of set questions to further their understanding of the occasion. The meal consists of three MATZAHS (unleavened bread) that represent the food of slavery and bitter herbs that represent the pain endured by the Jews in captivity. The herbs are dipped into condiments and *haroset* (a creamy sauce made of apples, nuts, cinnamon and a little wine). The condiments remind the participants that they are a free people but also remind them of the tears that have been shed in Egypt before their release. The *haroset* serves as symbol of the mortar used to construct the buildings of Egypt and also of the fruits of spring and thus hope. The other foods on the Seder plate are a roasted shank of lamb and a roasted egg, which serve to remind the participants of the ancient sacrifice that took place at the TEMPLE in JERUSALEM at Passover. Neither of these can be eaten. Four cups of wine are also drunk that represent the fourfold promise of salvation made by God in Exodus 6.6–7. A fifth cup of wine is kept but not drunk. It is symbolically poured for the prophet ELIJAH, who is due to herald the coming of the Messiah. Traditionally, the Seder meal is eaten in a reclining position. (*See also* MASSIACH; PESACH)

Sefardim *See* SEPHARDIM.

Sefer Torah The scrolls that contain the five books of the TORAH handwritten on parchment. Traditionally the scrolls are made of leather taken from an animal that Jews are allowed to eat. A special type of black ink is used and lines are ruled so that the Hebrew letters remain straight. The scribes who write the sacred script take about one year to complete one scroll. However, if any letter that is part of a divine name is written incorrectly, the scroll is not fit for use and the particular column has to be removed and buried. There are specific requirements for the text, such as writing certain letters with a crown or a dot above them, and some letters are written larger than others. The scrolls are kept in the ARK in the SYNAGOGUE and read in the services. (*See also* SIMCHAT TORAH)

Sefiroth   The ten attributes or emanations of the divine essence of God (AYN SOF) which, according to Jewish mysticism, join the celestial to the material world. They are sometimes depicted in visual form as the Tree of Life. The KETER (crown) is at the top of the tree. The left-hand descending branch contains BINAH (understanding), GERUVAH (power) and HOD (splendour); parallel to these on the right-hand branch are HOKHMAH (wisdom), HESED (lovingkindness) and NETZAH (victory). Descending straight down from *keter* are TIFERET (beauty), YESOD (foundation) and finally MALKHUT (beauty). This divine hierarchy is reflected in life on earth with the *sefiroth* on the left-hand side representing God's sternness, whilst those on the right express His mercy. Although we cannot comprehend the *ayn sof*, we can perceive the *sefiroth* at work in the creation and in human life.

Selihot   *Lit. pardon*. Penitential prayers recited during the YAMIM NORAIM and the period leading up to it.

Semikhah   *Lit. the laying on of hands*. The permission to provide a decision on matters of law which confers the title of RABBI to a man versed in Jewish law and practice. Traditionally, the right is passed on by teachers to their pupils. The idea of laying on of hands is traced back to MOSES, who gave leadership to JOSHUA by placing his hands on Joshua's head. In modern times, candidates for the rabbinate attend seminaries where they are awarded HATTURAT HORAAH. (*See also* KETAV SEMIKHAH; YESHIVA)

Sephardim / Sefardim   The Spanish Jews, including those that originate from around the Mediterranean or Middle East, as distinct from the ASHKENAZIM or German Jews. This twofold division of the Jewish people has existed for least one thousand years.

Seudah Shlishit   *Lit. the third meal.* A meal eaten at the end of the Sabbath, especially celebrated by HASIDIM and Jews who practise the KABBALA. The meal is accompanied by religious discussions and religious singing. (*See also* SHABBAT)

Seudath Mitzvah   *Lit. The Feast of Unleavened Bread.* An alternative name for the feast of Passover that refers to the unleavened bread prepared by the people of Israel before their rapid departure from slavery in Egypt. It is also used for the feast that is held on completion of a TORAH scroll or study of part of the TALMUD. (*See also* PESACH; SEDER; SIYYUM)

Shaatnez   *See* SHATNEZ.

Shabbat / Shabbos   The day of rest and renewal that is dedicated to the remembrance of God. It begins at sunset on Friday and finishes at nightfall on Saturday. The Sabbath day remembers the verses of GENESIS where God ceased the activity of creation and then sanctified the seventh day. The day provides the opportunity for the practising Jew to experience the sanctification of time by ceasing all work and therefore experiencing time as a simple gift of God. RABBIS have stated that the observation of the Sabbath is the equivalent to observance of the whole TORAH and that if all Jews were to observe one Sabbath correctly, the Messiah would return. The observation of the Sabbath is the fourth of the Ten Commandments, and it is believed that the beauty of the Sabbath pours out into the rest of the week. There are seven kinds of prohibited work that have been developed into 39 prohibitions. These are:
  1. The growing and preparation of food.
  2. The manufacture and preparation of clothing.
  3. Any work with leather or writing.
  4. Provision of shelter.
  5. Lighting or extinguishing fire.
  6. The completion of work already begun before the Sabbath.
  7. Transportation.
On the morning of the Sabbath, devout Jews will attend the SYNAGOGUE in order to hear the Torah read to remember the moment

of Revelation and this is usually the time that a BAR MITZVAH would take place. The meal that follows is similar to the meal that takes place on the Friday evening. The Sabbath afternoon is a time of relaxation but this will end with another visit to the synagogue where the first section of the following week's Torah reading will begin. The third meal will then take place but this one does not have the KIDDUSH. The regular evening service at the synagogue takes place but will end with the recitation of the HAVDALAH to solemnly end the Sabbath at nightfall. This will also be done at home by those not attending the synagogue. (*See also* EREV SHABBAT)

Shacharith   *See* SHAHARIT.

Shaddai   One of the names of God used instead of the unspoken YHVH.

Shaharit   The morning prayer and the first of the three obligatory daily prayers in which traditional Jews wear the TALLIT and TEFILLIN. God is thanked for the new day and PSALMS are recited in order to attune with the divine. The public worship consists of various blessings, the SHEMA and the AMIDAH. On some days the TORAH is read and on festival days the MUSSAF is added. (*See also* MAARIV; MINHAH)

Shaliah Tsibbur   A person chosen to lead the congregation in prayer.

Shalom   A word that indicates well-being such as happiness, peace, contentment, prosperity, good health or peace of mind. It is usually used by Jews as a greeting and farewell to each other when it is more formally combined with 'Aleikhem' to mean 'May the peace be with you.'

Shalom bayit   *Lit. domestic peace.* The term used to describe harmonious conjugal relations. Jewish rabbinical law lays down the necessary regulations to bring this about.

Shalosh Seudoth   *Lit. The Day of Delight.* A phrase taken from ISAIAH 58.13 to describe the Jewish Sabbath. (*See also* SHABBAT)

Shamir   A legendary worm believed to have been used by MOSES to engrave the names of the tribes of ISRAEL on the high priest's breast-plate. Later used by SOLOMON as an engraving tool when constructing the TEMPLE in JERUSALEM.

Shammash   The title used for a caretaker or sexton of a SYNAGOGUE. It is also used for the candle that lights the HANUKKAH candles.

Shatnez / Shaatnez   Clothes that contain a forbidden mixture of wool and linen and are not permitted to be worn by Orthodox Jews.

Shavuot   The Feast of Weeks celebrated 50 days after Passover on the sixth and seventh days of Sivan and also known as the Festival of the Wheat Harvest and the Day of the First Fruits. The two-day festival (one day in ISRAEL) remembers the revelation of the law to MOSES on Mount Sinai, although it probably originated as a harvest celebration. There are no special rituals and ceremonies, as it is believed that it is impossible to express the greatness of the revelation. However, it is customary to eat dishes made from dairy products. In recent times it has become the custom to decorate the SYNAGOGUE with plants and flowers which reflects the original harvest festival. Some traditional Jews will pass the night in the synagogue studying the TORAH. The synagogue service consists of prayers and poems that reflect both the revelation and the benefi-cence of nature. The reading from the Torah will include the passage that includes the Ten Commandments. The Book of RUTH is read on the second day. (*See also* BERIT; PESACH; SUKKOT)

Shechita / Shehitah   The ritual killing of animals that is carried out in accordance with the Jewish laws concerning food. Traditionally, the killing had to be performed by a skilled specialist who knew the religious law. Since the blood has to be removed from the meat, the animal's throat is slit and the blood allowed to drain. (*See also* HALLAP; KASHRUT; KOSHER; SHOHET)

Sheelot u-Teshuvot   A form of Jewish religious literature that appeared in the period of the SAVORAIM, the rabbinical commentators in

Babylon at the time of the Muslim invasion from the tenth century CE. Various questions on matters of law were put to the GEONIM, the heads of the Talmudic schools in Babylon, who provided answers often based on consensus. The decisions were based on their knowledge of the MISHNAH and the TALMUD and often there was fierce debate with other experts who disagreed. Many collections of these questions and answers were written down and became known as responsa literature or *Sheelot u-Teshuvot*.

Shehitah   *See* SHECHITA.

Sheitl   The wig traditionally worn by married women in ORTHODOX JUDAISM. The wig fulfils the requirement for Jewish women to cover their hair.

Shekhina / Shekhinah   The presence of God that is immanent in His creation. It is said that whenever Jews pray together the *shekhina* is present with them. It is also manifest within the heart of the pious Jew. RABBIS have described the *shekhina* as the glory of God, referred to as light. It is believed to be the manifestation of God that appears at the time of prophecy and revelation. Medieval rabbis argued that in the passages of the Bible where God is described in anthropomorphic terms, it is the *shekhina* that is being described.

Sheloshim   The period of 30 days of mourning that begins with the burial of a close relative. In the case of a parent it is extended to one full year. During this period the male mourner may not cut his hair or beard, attend festivities or marry. In the case of the death of a parent, the children attend the SYNAGOGUE every day for a year, both morning and evening, and recite the KADDISH. During this period the mourners do not visit the grave until the end of the year, when the tombstone is laid. (*See also* ANINUT; SHIVA; YAHRZEIT)

Shem ha-Gedolim   *Lit. names of the great*. A book written by Rabbi Azulai (1724–1806) in JERUSALEM that outlines the lives and works of great RABBIS.

Shema Three passages from the Book of DEUTERONOMY in the Jewish Scriptures that begin 'Hear O Israel, the Lord is our God, the Lord is One.' This affirmation of monotheism and election is recited at the time of morning and evening prayer and is written inside the MEZUZAH that are fixed to the doorposts of Jewish homes. They are also contained in the TEFILLIN that are strapped on the body during prayer. They have become virtually the article or essence of the Jewish faith and many devout Jews will utter them as their last words before death. The full rendering is as follows:

Hear O Israel, the Lord is our God, the Lord is One
Blessed be His glorious Kingdom forever and ever!
Love you then the Lord your God
With all heart, with all your soul, with all your might!
Take to heart these words, which I command you this day,
Impress them upon your children
By speaking about them
When you sit in your home and when you walk by the way,
When you lie down and when you rise up;
Bind them as a sign upon your hand
And let them serve as frontlets between your eyes,
Inscribe them on the doorposts of your house
And upon your gates.

(*See also* BERIT; TEFILLAH)

Shemini Atzerat The final two days of the feast of SUKKOT are the Eighth Day of Assembly (*Shemini Atzerat*) and SIMCHAT TORAH, but in ISRAEL both festivals are held on one day. At the Day of Assembly prayers are recited for rain.

Shemoneh Esre *See* AMIDAH.

Sheol *See* GEHENNA.

Shiddukh *Lit. marital match*. The term used traditionally for betrothal or marriage. It comes from the Talmudic reference to conversations between prospective bridegrooms and the bride or her parents in preparation for betrothal.

Shir ha-Kavod A hymn of praise sung by ASHKENAZI Jews during the morning service at the SYNAGOGUE. During its recitation the ARK is opened.

Shir ha-Maalot The title found at the head of each of the PSALMS from 124 to 134, translated as 'The Song of Degrees'. The title's significance is obscure and it is speculated that the 'Ascent', indicated by the idea of 'degrees', may refer to the recitation by pilgrims on the way to JERUSALEM or Jews returning from exile in Babylon.

Shir ha-Shirim The Hebrew title for the Song of Songs, a scriptural book which is part of the HAGIOGRAPHA. It is commonly believed to have been written by SOLOMON and consists of love poetry. Traditional Jewish commentators believe the poetry to be allegorical for the love between God and ISRAEL.

Shirayim Food left over by the TZADDIK at the Sabbath or festival meal. It is highly desired and competed for by the HASIDIM who attend. It is believed that such food shares in the blessings conferred upon the *tzaddik* in his role as intermediary between man and God.

Shishah Sedarim The arrangement of the MISHNAH into six sections known as 'orders'. They are Zeraim, Moed, Nashim, Nezikin, Kadashim and Tohcrot.

Shiva / Shivah The first seven days of deepest mourning following the death of a close relative, taking place immediately after the funeral. Traditionally, the mourner returns home and covers all mirrors and lights a lamp in honour of the deceased. The mourner removes leather shoes and sits on the ground or uses a low stool. It is forbidden to cut the hair, shave or indulge in sexual relations. Even study of the TORAH ceases. However, comfort is available from relatives and friends; the first meal after the funeral is made by close friends and is traditionally eggs or lentils, the symbols of mourning. A service takes place in the house every morning and evening. (*See also* ANINUT; KERIAH; SHELOSHIM)

Shnoder   A Yiddish word used to describe the act of making an offering to the SYNAGOGUE.

Shoah   The systematic genocide of six million Jews by the Nazi regime during the Second World War.

Shofar   The ram's horn which has been used on special religious occasions since biblical times. It is believed to have accompanied the revelation on Mount Sinai and was blown at the start of battle or after victory. It is said that the shofar will sound on the coming of the Messiah. It is also blown at the Jewish New Year (ROSH HASHANAH) and at the end of YOM KIPPUR.

Shohet   A ritual slaughterer of animals. Although the TALMUD dictates that any adult person may kill animals as long as the requirements of Jewish law are maintained, in the modern period the person is properly trained and is also expected to be learned in Jewish law or HALAKHAH. (*See also* KASHRUT; SHECHITA)

Shomer   *Lit. watcher.* The supervisor of KASHRUT who is appointed to oversee and inspect the preparation of food in slaughterhouses, restaurants and other public outlets.

Shtetl   *Lit. a little town.* A Yiddish term now used to describe the lost world of East European jewry destroyed by the Holocaust.

Shul   A Yiddish word used by ASHKENAZI Jews for a SYNAGOGUE.

Shulhan Arukh   *Lit. the set table.* The authoritative code of Jewish law as elaborated by Joseph Caro (1488–1575). During the period of the GEONIM (the heads of the schools of law in Babylon), from the time of the rise of Islam to the eleventh century, it had become the custom to provide answers to questions posed by Jews concerning points of law. These generated vast written collections known as responsa. It then became necessary to organize the responsa into a systematic collection. The authoritative collections are the *Shulhan Arukh* and the *Mishnah Torah*. The *Shulhan Arukh* is divided into four sections as follows: *The Path of Life*, which deals with worship and festivals; *The Teacher of Knowledge*, which is concerned with ethics, charitable duties, dietary laws and mourning; *The Stone of Help*, which deals with marriage; and *The Breastplate of Judgement*, which covers civil law. (*See also* MISHNAH; SAVORAIM; SHEELOT U-TESHUVOT)

Shushan Purim   The celebration on the feast of PURIM on the 15th day of the month of Adar (February–March) instead of the usual 14th day. This is a requirement for cities whose ancient walls date back to the time of JOSHUA, such as JERUSALEM. It is celebrated in remembrance of the Jews of Shushan who began to fight on the 14th but achieved victory on the 15th.

Siddur   The daily prayer book which contains the order of service held in the SYNAGOGUE. The first written arrangement of Jewish liturgy was made by Rabbi Amram (d. 875), one of the GEONIM of Sura. However, the essentials of the synagogue service were probably known from around the sixth century. (*See also* AMIDAH; HAFTARAH; SHAHARIT; SHEMA)

Sidrah   The part of the TORAH read in the SYNAGOGUE on the Sabbath. Each *sidrah* is named after the first important word found in the text. The five books of the *sidrah* are divided into 54 readings so that the entirety is read annually. (*See also* SHABBAT)

Sifra   The exposition of the Book of LEVITICUS, also known as Torah Kohanim, that is one of the three writings that form the MIDRASH. (*See also* MEKHILTA; SIFRE)

Sifre   The exposition of the Books of NUMBERS and DEUTERONOMY that is one of the three writings that form the MIDRASH. (*See also* MEKHILTA; SIFRA)

Simchat Bet ha-Shoevah   *Lit. festival of the water drawing.* A festival that was observed at the completion of the first day of SUKKOT. Traditionally water was poured, bonfires were lit and there was dancing and singing. The festival has not been celebrated since the destruction of the Second TEMPLE.

Simchat Torah / Simhat Torah *Lit. Rejoicing in the Torah.* The ninth day and completion of the festival of SUKKOT, and the day on which the annual cycle of TORAH readings is completed and begins anew. It is a happy occasion in which the Torah scrolls are removed from the ARK in the SYNAGOGUE and carried around in procession by the congregation. Thirteen-year-old boys are called to read from the Torah, together with an adult who recites the blessing. (*See also* SEFER TORAH)

Siyyum *Lit. termination.* A term applied to the successful completion of a TORAH scroll or the study of part of the TALMUD. In celebration of these events a special feast is held with a concluding lecture. (*See also* SEUDATH MITZVAH)

Sod *Lit. secret.* An esoteric method utilizing allegory for the exegesis of sacred texts. It is used primarily by those involved in KABBALA and is based on the belief that the TORAH has more than one level of meaning.

Solomon The son of DAVID and king of ISRAEL. He developed the absolute monarchy begun by David and brought about economic, social and cultural changes to Hebrew society. The kingdom was divided into 12 provinces under the control of the central state situated in JERUSALEM. The state of Israel became rich and powerful and took part in the diplomatic life of the Middle East. Solomon married the daughters of surrounding rulers, including the Pharaoh's. Trade and cultural exchanges also took place with the surrounding area and the TEMPLE and palace in Jerusalem reflect the influence of Phoenician architecture. Some leaders were disturbed by the new wealth and the outside cultural influences, and after Solomon's death the kingdom divided into two. However, Solomon is usually regarded as a repository of wisdom and the author of the Song of Songs and the Book of ECCLESIASTES, eventually accepted as part of the Jewish canon of Scripture.

Succoth   See SUKKOT.

Sukkah   A temporary shelter constructed by Jewish families, in which meals are eaten during the festival of SUKKOT. The booths are three-sided structures covered with foliage or things that grow from the soil. They are decorated with hangings and pictures. The *sukkah* are constructed to remember the temporary dwellings built by the Jews whilst wandering in the Sinai desert after release from Egypt. It is also stated that they should remind the Jews of the transience of all things.

Sukkot / Sukkoth   One of the three important festivals celebrated in Judaism and known as the Feast of Tabernacles. It is held for eight days (seven in Israel) during the month of Tishrie (6 September – 4 October), a few days after YOM KIPPUR. The festival remembers the care taken by God during the wandering after release from bondage in Egypt and contains two distinctive ceremonies. The first is the making and waving of four interwoven branches of the palm, citron, myrtle and willow known as the ARBA MINIM. The second is the creation of SUKKAH, that is, booths or temporary shelters made of foliage to replicate the temporary homes made by the people of Israel when they travelled for forty years in the desert before arriving at the Promised Land. The festival includes the three sacred days of HOSHANA RABBA, SHEMINI ATZERAT, and SIMCHAT TORAH.

Synagogue   The Jewish meeting place for communal prayer, instruction and social activities that probably became prominent after the destruction of the second TEMPLE by the Romans in 70 CE. The Talmudic RABBIS insisted that for certain occasions, such as the repetition of the KADDISH, the KEDUSHAH, the AMIDAH and the readings from the TORAH scrolls, a MINYAN of ten adult male Jews was required. They also stated that communal prayer was more important than individual prayer. For both these reasons the synagogue came to play a central role in Jewish worship. The archi-tectural rules for the sacred space are simple: the building should contain an ARK in the east wall to contain the Torah scrolls and there should be a raised platform from which the Torah can be read. The building should also contain windows. Everything else is at the discretion of the congregation and the architect. (*See also* BET HA-TEFILLAH; BIMAH; SEFER TORAH)

T

Tachanun   Part of the traditional funeral arrangements, in which the washing and clothing of the deceased is performed by the HEVRAH KADISHAH, a local body of Jews who serve the dying and the dead. (*See also* TAHARAH; TAKHRIKHIM)

Tahanun   The prayer for grace and forgiveness recited daily, except on the Sabbath and festival days, after the morning and afternoon AMIDAH.

Taharah   The washing of the body that takes place before the dressing in preparation for the funeral. This function is traditionally carried out by the HEVRAH KADISHAH, a local body of Jews who serve the dying and the dead. The body is washed in lukewarm water through a sheet placed on top of it. The nails are cut and the hair is groomed. (*See also* TACHANUN; TAKHRIKHIM; TUMAH)

Takhrikhim   Traditional Jewish garments in which the dead are buried. After washing, the body is dressed in a white cap, shirt, trousers, linen shoes and the KITTEL worn on YOM KIPPUR, then wrapped in a white shroud. Finally a TALLIT is placed in the coffin, resting over the deceased shoulders as worn in life. (*See also* HEVRAH KADISHAH; TACHANUN; TAHARAH)

Takkanot / Takkanah   A decree issued by the community or a regulation supplementing the law as laid down in the TORAH.

Tallit / Tallith   A four-cornered white prayer shawl with fringes worn by Orthodox men at morning prayers and on the Day of Atonement (YOM KIPPUR). It is also placed in the coffin over the shoulders of the corpse. The *tallit* is seen as a robe of responsibility that marks the Jew out as someone who is accountable in every action, whether in the home or at work. It allows the Jew to remember his/her special relationship with God. There is no restriction in the size of a *tallit* but it should be white, possess four corners and on each of the corners there must a fringe or tassel. One of the tassles should be blue. (*See also* ATTARAH; ZIZIT)

Tallith Katan   *See* ARBA KANFOT.

Talmud   The main source of Jewish law, it contains the MISHNAH and the GEMARA. The former is a collection of the oral law compiled by the second century CE. The latter comprises rabbinic commentaries on the Mishnah written between 200 and 500. By the first half of the fourth century, Jewish scholars had collected together the teachings of generations of RABBIS who had lived in the great centres of study in Palestine. This work became known as the Palestinian Talmud. However, parallel developments had taken place in Babylon with the opening of several influential schools of learning. As the institutions in ISRAEL went into decline, the Babylonian schools took over and produced their own collections of interpretations of the Mishnah, known as the Babylonian Talmud. The Talmud goes further than the Mishnah, in that it contains debates between rabbis, theology, philosophy and ethics. (*See also* TORAH)

Tanakh / Tenakh   The 24 books of the Jewish Scriptures which together form the TORAH, NEVIIM and KETUVIM. There is a hierarchy of sanctity associated with the books: the five books that comprise the Torah are the most sacred as they are the direct revelation of God to MOSES and provide the law that binds Jews to God in a holy covenant; the books that comprise the writings of the prophets (neviim) are next in orders of sacredness; and the books known as Holy Writings (ketuvim) are believed to have been written through inspiration rather than revelation.

Tanhuma A Palestinian MIDRASH collection which covers the entire five books attributed to MOSES. It is usually believed to be authored by Tanhuma bar Abba.

Tannaim The term used for the rabbinical commentators on the Scriptures who lived before 200 CE and prior to the editing of the MISHNAH. The same term is also used for the agreed conditions that traditionally were drawn up when a Jewish couple entered their formal engagement to be married. (*See also* AMORAIM)

Tanya A Hasidic kabbalistic book written by Shnoeur Zalman, which guides the adherent in the attainment of DEVEKUT. (*See also* HASIDIM; KABBALA)

Tappuhim *Lit. apples.* The fruit-shaped ornamental work used to decorate the staves of the TORAH scrolls.

Targum The name given to any translation of the TORAH or single book of the TANAKH into Aramaic. The practice became established in the Second TEMPLE period.

Tashlikh A traditional prayer of repentance observed on the afternoon of ROSH HASHANAH, which the people should say by a river bank.

Tashmishei kedushah Religious objects that are part of the liturgy practised in the SYNAGOGUE and which usually include the TALLIT, the SHOFAR and the TORAH ornaments.

Tebah In Sephardic usage, a raised platform in the SYNAGOGUE. (*See also* BIMAH; SEPHARDIM)

Techinah A prayer book especially for women used by Orthodox Jews, and written in Yiddish, which provides instructions on how to pray.

Tefillah / Tefila The term for all Jewish prayer and meditation. Prayer is regarded as a communication from the heart overflowing into words. The prayers may be calls for forgiveness, repentance or petition. In Judaism, while individual prayer is important, communal prayer has precedence, as the community in prayer is a microcosm of the covenant between God and His chosen people. After the ritual communal prayer, Jews may offer their individual petitions. Prayers may be in any language, but Hebrew is regarded as the sacred language. The prayer is structured and there is a fixed liturgy for the three-times-daily prayer. The set prayers require the Orthodox Jew to don the TALLIT and the TEFILLIN.

Tefillin / Tephillin / T'filin   Small leather boxes or phylacteries that contain four passages from the TORAH (EXODUS 13.1–10; 11–16; DEUTERONOMY 6.4–9; 11.13–21) that place emphasis on the unity of God, divine rule and redemption from Egypt. One is tied to the forehead and another to the forearm of Jewish men when they recite the morning prayers. The commandment in the Torah to wear the tefillin is regarded as one of the three outward signs of Judaism, along with the MEZUZAH and the ZIZIT. (*See also* TEFILLAH)

Tehillim   The Hebrew term for the Book of PSALMS, one of the books of the Hebrew Scriptures that forms part of the Holy Writings (KETUVIM). The Psalms are sung to music in the SYNAGOGUE on many occasions in the Jewish religious calendar. Most of the songs express the glory of God and ask for forgiveness and mercy and extol the qualities of God. Of the 150 Psalms, 73 are attributed to DAVID.

Tehinnah   *Lit. supplication.* A private devotional prayer or a prayer written for private use. These prayers may include those recited for forgiveness, blessings and protection and for success in studying the TORAH. There exist devotional books written in both Yiddish and vernacular languages which include prayers for the sick, prayers at a cemetery, blessings for children and prayers for use when baking Sabbath cakes or lighting Sabbath candles. Devotional books written for women were also known as *tehinnot*.

Temple   The First Temple was built by Solomon in Jerusalem in the tenth century BCE and became the first permanent structure to hold the ARK OF THE COVENANT. It served as the central site for prayer and the place of communal sacrifices that were held daily. At Passover, all families were obliged to attend for the paschal sacrifice. In the sixth century BCE, the First Temple was destroyed by the Assyrians when they invaded ISRAEL. On the return of the Jews at the end of the century, permission was granted to rebuild the Temple and this site was maintained until destroyed by the Romans in 70 CE. The only surviving part of the Temple is the wall that backs on to the Muslim mosque of Al-Aqsa in JERUSALEM and is known as the Wailing Wall. This is a famous site of Jewish prayer in the old quarter of the city. Although the SYNAGOGUE was introduced by the Jews who were in captivity at the time of the destruction of the First Temple, and is now the mainstay of Jewish congregational prayers, most traditional Jews still hope for the restoration of the Temple in Jerusalem when the Messiah returns.

Tenakh   *See* TANAKH.

Tephillin   *See* TEFILLIN

Terefah   A term used to describe non-KOSHER food. (*See also* KASHRUT)

Teruah   Hebrew term for a blast on the SHOFAR. Thus the festival of ROSH HASHANAH, where the shofar is blown, is alternatively called Yom Teruah.

Teshuvah   *Lit. return.* Repentance or returning to God which is considered to be a daily obligation by devout Jews. The action of repentance should consist of remorse, confession and correction. Words of repentance are part of the three daily prayers. There is also a season of the year put aside for repentance which begins at the month of ELLUL (8 August – 6 September) with the daily blowing of the SHOFAR. Several days before the feast of ROSH HASHANAH in the following month of Tishrie, penitential prayers begin. The week after Rosh Hashanah is known as the Days of Repentance but it is YOM KIPPUR, or the Day of Atonement, that is most associated with the act of repentance.

Tevilah The full immersion into water in the presence of a rabbinical court that is required by Jewish law as part of the ritual of conversion and followed by Orthodox Jews.

T'fillin *See* TEFILLIN.

Tiferet *Lit. beauty*. According to the tradition of the KABBALA, the sixth of the ten SEFIROTH who emanate from the AYN SOF. It is the second in the central trunk of the Tree of Life and is the harmonizing principle between love and power, an essential balance that is required for the world to exist.

Tikkun A night vigil maintained by traditional Jews, especially those who practise KABBALA. It is also used to describe collections of PSALMS, lamentations, and petitions used on such occasions, often recited in memory of the destruction of the TEMPLE.

Tikkun Olam / Tikun Care for the world or stewardship of the Earth. In traditional Judaism this would arise from the words in GENESIS which indicate that mankind has been entrusted with stewardship over all the plants and animals. The mystical tradition has posited the idea that TIKKUN is a task of cosmic repair that restores the creation to harmony with God. This may be achieved by maintaining all of God's commandments. (*See also* KABBALA; TORAH)

Tish A meal observed in the Hasidic tradition, held on the Sabbath, holidays and the anniversaries of the deaths of Hasidic spiritual leaders. The meal is eaten in the company of the TZADDIK, the spiritual leader of the community. Followers will sing hymns with him and partake in the leftovers of his food. On the Sabbath, the meal will end with dancing. (*See also* HASIDIM; SHIRAYIM)

Tishah B'Av A fast day held on the ninth day of Av (9 July – 7 August) known as 'the black fast' as it commemorates the destruction of the TEMPLE. The fast lasts from evening to evening and begins with a mourning meal of eggs and bread dipped in ashes. Leather shoes are removed until the fast is completed. The SYNAGOGUE is dimly lit and the worship is performed as if the congregation were was in mourning. The Book of LAMENTATIONS is read at the service. On the second day it is not permitted to wash; the TORAH reading is taken from DEUTERONOMY and after the reading the congregation sings dirges until noon, which recount all the tragedies that have befallen the Jewish people. With the rising of the moon and appearance of the stars, the fast ends.

Tobit A central figure in a Jewish apocryphal book of the same name. (*See also* APOCRYPHA)

Toladot The specific actions that are forbidden on the SHABBAT under the heading of each of the 39 categories of labour known as AB.

Torah The term used for the first five books of the Jewish Scriptures, which incorporate the law of God provided in the revelation given to MOSES. The books are GENESIS, EXODUS, DEUTERONOMY, LEVITICUS and NUMBERS. However, the RABBIS have written extensive commentaries and interpretations that include the concept of an oral Torah that was passed on to Moses but not written down, in which God fully explained the written Torah. The term *Torah* is therefore enlarged to include the written Torah, the other books of the Jewish Scriptures, the MISHNAH and the TALMUD – in other words, the full canopy of Jewish teaching, the complete picture of God's commandments as elaborated and understood through Jewish history. (*See also* SEFER TORAH)

Torah Kohanim *See* SIFRA.

Trefa Food that is forbidden to Jews by their dietary laws and is not KOSHER. (*See also* KASHRUT)

Tumah The condition of impurity of a dead body that makes it unclean for those that touch it or live in the same house where the body is kept. Among Orthodox Jewry, a member of the KOHANIM may not attend the cemetery or be a member of the HEVRAH KADISHAH, the professional body that cares of the dead and dying. (*See also* TAHARAH)

Tzaddik / Tzedak   A just or righteous person who loves God and the TORAH and practises good deeds. According to Judaism, the aspiration to be a *tzaddik* should be the goal of all Jews. In the Hasidic movement, the *tzaddik* is a spiritual leader regarded as the intermediary between humans and God, who can bring down divine blessings. He is visited for his wisdom and practical advice on daily and spiritual matters and on the Sabbath and at festivals, large numbers of HASIDIM will gather to share a meal with him. (*See also* SHIRAYIM; TZEDAKAH)

Tzedakah   The striving to be a righteous person by acquiring such virtues as truthfulness, uprightness, piety, honesty and justice. The most effective way to practise *tzedakah* would be to obey the TORAH through a single-minded love of God. In popular usage the term refers to an act of charity. Jews are famous for their charitable acts, but they should be performed with joyfulness and with respect for the recipient. (*See also* TZADDIK)

Tzeniut   *Lit. modesty.* A term describing the code of modest behaviour and dress required particularly from women in traditional Judaism.

Tzizit / Tzittzit   *See* ZIZIT.

Tzom Gedaliah   The day that follows ROSH HASHANAH and is used as a fast to commemorate Gedaliah, a pious Jew murdered by his fellow Jews after being appointed Governor of Judah by the Babylonians. The fast is used to reinforce the ethical teaching that one should not blame others for one's own misfortunes but instead use them as an occasion to examine oneself.

V

Ve-hu rahum *Lit. And he, being merciful.* The opening words of verse 38 of PSALM 78 used in the Jewish prayer book as the introduction to the daily evening service.

Viddui Confession of sins declared on YOM KIPPUR or on one's deathbed.

Y

Yad   A pointer held in the hand when reading from the TORAH in the SYNAGOGUE. Any damage to the Torah scrolls makes them *patul* or unusable. Thus, every care is taken to avoid damaging the text, and for this reason the readers do not mark their place in the text with their fingers as this may cause smudging of the ink.

Yahadut   The religion of the Jewish people known as Judaism that believes in one God who has chosen ISRAEL by giving the people His TORAH so that they may be an example to humanity, and so that the presence of God may be amongst humanity. As a consequence of its covenant with God to obey His law as revealed in the Torah, the emphasis of Judaism is on orthopraxy rather than orthodoxy, but belief also plays an important role. (*See also* YEHUDIM)

Yahrzeit   The anniversary of a parent's death. A candle is lit from evening to evening and the offspring of the deceased may fast on the day. They would be expected to visit the SYNAGOGUE and recite the KADDISH and spend some time studing the TORAH. The grave is visited, prayers are said, and a small stone left on the grave. (*See also* ANINUT; KERIAH; SHELOSHIM; SHIVAH; YIZKOR)

Yahweh   The name given to the God that is not expressible and usually depicted as YHWH if it needs to be written. This name has not been spoken since the exile and is usually substituted by other names such as ADONAI.

Yamim Noraim   The ten days of repentance in the month of Tishrie (6 September – 4 October) that begin with ROSH HASHANAH and end with YOM KIPPUR and are considered the most sacred in the Jewish calendar. It is a time for forgiveness and repentance both before God and one's fellow human beings.

Yamulkah   The Yiddish term for the small skullcap worn by Jewish men. (*See also* KIPPAH)

Yehudim   The Hebrew term for a Jew. Jewishness is traditionally defined by matrilineal descent – a child of a Jewish mother is a Jew. However, this is complicated by two factors: in 1983, the Central Conference of American Rabbis, a REFORM gathering, determined that a child of either a Jewish mother or a Jewish father can be deemed a Jew if brought up in an environment that leads to identification with the Jewish people; second, it is possible to convert to Judaism. The important point here is that Jewishness is not defined by religiosity; however, Judaism is the religion of the Jewish people. (*See also* YAHADUT)

Yerusalem   *See* JERUSALEM.

Yeshiva / Yeshivah   A college for the study of the TORAH and the TALMUD. Although Jewish males had always engaged in study of the Torah under the guidance of their RABBIS, in the nineteenth century organized colleges appeared in Eastern Europe which allowed progression through the various stages of study. Secular study was not permitted and some students spent a lifetime in study of the Torah, Talmud and HALAKHAH.

Yesod   *Lit. foundation.* According to the tradition of the KABBALA, the ninth of the ten SEFIROTH who emanate from the AYN SOF. It is the third in the central trunk of the Tree of Life and is the means by which God's light flows into the MALKHUT and then into creation.

Yetser   The human inclination or impulse to either good (*yetser ha-tov*) or evil (*yetser ha-ra*) that is part of human nature. There is no doctrine of original sin in Judaism.

Yiddish   The constructed language made up of German, Russian and other East European languages, used by the ASHKENAZI in the DIASPORA and still spoken by many Orthodox Jews, even in ISRAEL. Hebrew is maintained as a sacred language, although it is spoken by most other Israelis. (*See also* IVRIT)

Yigdal   *Lit. May God be magnified.* The hymn sung at the culmination of the Sabbath and festival evening services and based upon the 13 principles of MAIMONIDES.

Yihud   In Orthodox Jewish weddings, the practice of taking the couple to a room in the building and leaving them alone. The door of the room will be guarded by the witnesses to the marriage. The announcement is made to the guests that the couple are breaking their fast, but the reason is so that the marriage can be consummated, thereby fulfilling one of the three ways of entering a marriage contract. (*See also* KETUBAH)

Yihus   Achieving distinction. Although this could be obtained by distinguished ancestry or right marriage, the correct way to obtain distinction was through one's lifestyle as a practising Jew. The Jew who gave to charity, studied the TORAH, fulfilled all their religious duties and brought up children in the knowledge and practice of the Torah was considered to possess yihus. In this way the community in exile was able to combat any forces that weakened or diluted the practice of Judaism in exile.

Yisrael   *See* ISRAEL.

Yizkor   A special memorial service observed on the final day of the pilgrimage festivals (PESACH, SHAVUOT, SUKKOT) and YOM KIPPUR in order to remember the recently departed in front of the congregation. (*See also* YAHRZEIT)

Yom Ha-Atzmaut   The day set aside to celebrate the founding of the modern state of ISRAEL, or Independence Day. It is celebrated on 14 May.

Yom Hashoah The day which is set aside to commemorate the SHOAH and remember the 6 million Jewish martyrs that were massacred by the Nazi regime in Germany. It is held on the 27th day of the month of Nissan that falls between mid-March and mid-April. (*See also* SHOAH)

Yom Kippur The Day of Atonement that occurs ten days after ROSH HASHANAH, the New Year. The ten days in between are known as the Days of Penitence and used to re-examine one's life. This period culminates in Yom Kippur, the most solemn of the Jewish holy days, which is maintained by fasting and refraining from sexual intercourse. The ARK is draped in white and traditionally many of the congregation at the SYNAGOGUE will also wear white. Although it is a time to ask for God's forgiveness, it is not only a confession of sin, but also a day of reconciliation between God and His people. The vigil begins on the eve of Yom Kippur, and the evening service is the only time when everyone wears the TALLIT. After the arrival of the TORAH scrolls, the cantor will chant the KOL NIDREI three times. The Yom Kippur service consists of confessions in the morning with readings from the Torah followed by the HAFTARAH, the reading from the Book of Prophets taken from ISAIAH where the motivations for fasting are revealed; the MUSSAF, the extra prayer only performed on festival days; and the second Torah reading. The Mussaf prayer service will include a memorial to Jewish martyrs and recently dead friends and relatives. The concluding prayer, known as the NEILAH, is only performed on this occasion and is recited with great fervour. During the evening service, the emphasis is on reaffirmation of faith and ends with blast of the SHOFAR.

Yom Kippur Katan A miniature form of YOM KIPPUR, introduced by the mystics of Safat to purge the soul of arrogance and pride, that is celebrated in the SYNAGOGUE before the feast of the new moon. (*See also* ROSH HODESH)

Yomtov *Lit. days of celebration.* This term is used collectively to describe the Jewish festivals that always commemorate great events in Jewish history. The principal festivals are PESACH, SHAVUOT, SUKKOT, YOM KIPPUR, HANUKKAH, PURIM and ROSH HASHANAH.

Yomtov Sheni   The practice of observing a second holy day when only one is prescribed in the TORAH. This has become normal observance except in the case of YOM KIPPUR when the RABBIS ruled that two days' fasting would be too arduous. The idea of observing a second day arose out of uncertainty about when a festival should begin, when communities in DIASPORA were far from decisions made in the SANHEDRIN in JERUSALEM.

Z

Zaddikim   *Lit. righteous ones.* The leaders of the HASIDIM who are believed to be in a state of closeness or proximity to God at all times. The Hasidic Jew is expected to find a *zaddik* or REBBE to act as a guide and a counsellor in order to bring him/her closer to the divine. There are now several famous dynasties of *zaddiks* such as the Lubavitch, Sotmar, Ger and Bobov, who have passed on their leadership for several generations. The *zaddiks* have produced over 3,000 works that supplement the traditional Jewish canon of scripture.

Zechariah   One of the 12 minor prophets and a book of the Jewish Scriptures of the same name. Zechariah prophesied and preached around 520 BCE. He was a contemporary of HAGGAI and emphasized spiritual and righteous living over and above material power such as wealth or physical prowess. (*See also* NEVIIM)

Zeman Herutenu   *Lit. the season of our freedom.* One of the names given to the festival of Passover (PESACH). It refers to the deliverance of the Hebrew tribes from slavery in Egypt through the intervention of God and their eventual emergence as a separate nation with their own land in ISRAEL. (*See also* BERIT)

Zemirot   Table songs traditionally sung to enliven the meal eaten at the Sabbath.

Zephaniah   One of the 12 minor prophets and a book of the Jewish Scriptures of the same name. A contemporary of JEREMIAH, he warned the people that the time of final judgement by God was inevitable and therefore to display humility and live a righteous life. (*See also* NEVIIM)

Zikhron Teruah   The reference to the memorial blowing of a ram's horn (SHOFAR) in the Book of LEVITICUS in the Jewish Scriptures that is repeated annually on the feast of the Jewish New Year. (*See also* ROSH HASHANAH)

Zikhronot   A proclamation that God is the Master of absolute Remembrance and Judge of the Universe that is made on the feast of ROSH HASHANAH, the Jewish New Year. (*See also* MUSSAF)

Zionism   The movement founded by Theodore Hertzl in 1897 to establish a Jewish state in Palestine. Although Jews in the DIASPORA had always prayed to return to JERUSALEM, the hope of return was bound up with Messianic expectations. Increasingly, under the pressure of anti-Semitism in Eastern Europe and Russia, non-religious groups began to campaign for a Jewish homeland as the only solution to persecution. At the end of the nineteenth century, the first Zionist Congress was held, after which leaders began a campaign to persuade the British authorities to hand over Palestine to the Jews. After the Second World War, the creation of a Jewish state became the approved policy of the United Nations. Eventually, the Zionists achieved their aim in 1948. However, there has always been conflict with Orthodox Jews, who believe that ISRAEL should be a religious state implementing the TORAH (Jewish law) in its entirety.

Ziporah   The wife of the prophet MOSES, and daughter of JETHRO, the priest of Midian.

Zizit / Tzizit / Tzittzit   The fringes which are required to be at the four borders of Jewish garments according to the instructions in the TORAH. Today, Orthodox Jews maintain the fringes of wool or silk on each of the four corners of their prayer shawls. It is also used for the fringed undervest worn by Orthodox males. (*See also* ARBA KANFOT).

Zohar The most important text of Jewish mysticism, sometimes called the Bible of the KABBALA, written in the thirteenth century and attributed to Moses de Leon of Spain. This work has been highly influential on later scholars and mystics of the kabbala tradition, especially those of the Safat school in Palestine. A verse-by-verse commentary on the five books of the PENTATEUCH written in Aramaic, it attempts to provide a deeper allegorical understanding that reveals the nature of God.